M000199106

The Tarot
life planner
change your destiny & enrich your life

The Tarot
life planner
change your destiny & enrich your life

Lady Lorelei

GODSFIELD

For Harry Edward Michael I, who has always inspired me by example, Harry Edward Michael II, who encourages me with enthusiasm, and Harry Edward Michael III, who entrances me with life!

Special thanks to Sarah Tomley for editing this and *Gypsy Fortunes*; special thanks to Mom for having tarot decks in the house; very special thanks to D. Melissa Averett, Attorney at Law, Champion of the Downtrodden, Executive Director of Domestic Violence Civil Legal Services Inc. – she knows why.

An Hachette UK company
www.hachette.co.uk

This edition published in 2022 by Godsfield,
an imprint of Octopus Publishing Group
Carmelite House, 50 Victoria Embankment
London, EC4y 0DZ
www.octopusbooks.co.uk

ISBN 978-1-841-81517-6

A CIP catalogue record for this book is available from the British Library

Printed and bound in China

10 9 8 7 6 5 4 3 2 1

Publisher: Lucy Pessell
Designer: Hannah Coughlin
Editor: Sarah Kennedy
Editorial Assistant: Emily Martin
Senior Production Manager: Peter Hunt

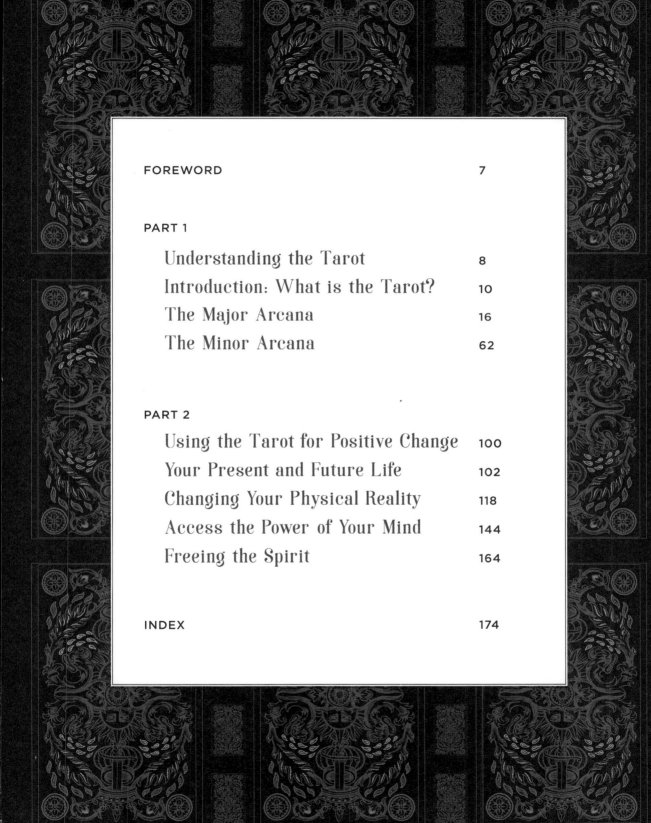

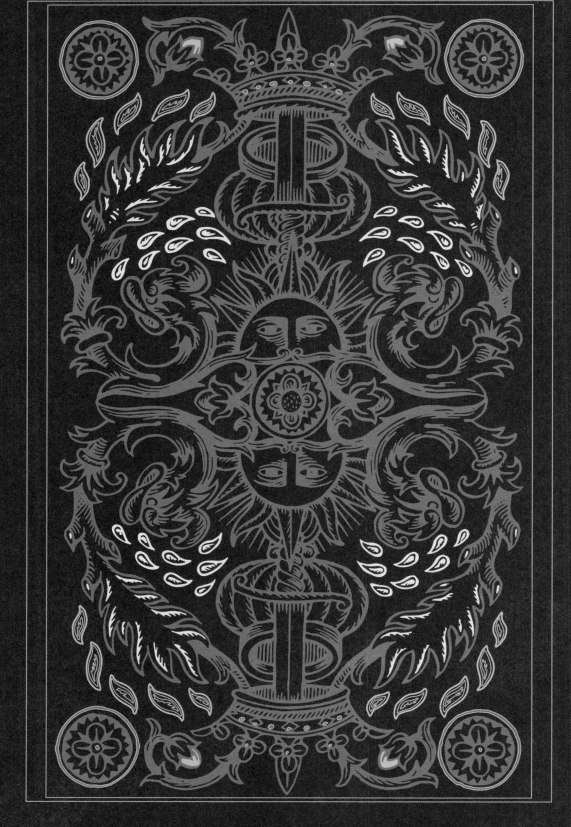

Foreword

I have always been fascinated by the occult and the power of the mind, but as my mother once said, 'We don't talk about that sort of thing in our family.' So I didn't delve into it until long after I was out on my own, after ten years living as a nun in a Vedic temple, following an electrical engineering degree. After that and more, I came full circle, bought a tarot deck and started looking into who I am.

That was around 1997 and since then I have discovered that the tarot is a great tool for self-examination and life planning. I'm not psychic: I can't read minds or talk to dead people, or predict the future any more accurately than common sense has always allowed me. Any ability I have to read the tarot – for myself and other people – is a result of my wide-ranging life experience and the effort I have put into understanding reality, both physical and metaphysical.

I remember a character in a science-fiction book who started off in the military, gave it all up to become a monk, then was recruited to lead a mission to the stars. He reinvented himself every time. It's an idea that resonates strongly with me. I once had a life plan to be an engineer, but I changed direction in an effort to find happiness and keep life interesting. Now I find myself teaching tarot and rescuing feral kittens. Next... well, who knows?

My purpose in writing this book is to share the many uses I have found for the tarot and encourage you to use it to reinvent yourself, just as I have, to get closer to the person you really are. My point of view is highly personal and spiritual. I sometimes refer to my experience of the tarot as a communication with God or Goddess. This isn't intended to exclude any particular religion or those with no religion. It's simply the way I use language. This book is about the way I use the tarot. There is no right or wrong way. Listen to your own wisdom as you read and work through the exercises.

Part One
Understanding the Tarot

The traditional tarot deck is made up of 78 picture cards, of which 56 are minor arcana, comprising four suits (Wands, Cups, Swords and Coins) of 14 cards each, and 22 are trumps or major arcana that have no suit designation. Modern 52-card playing decks are the minor arcana minus the Page. Tarot cards were originally used for gaming and gambling, but at some point became used for fortune telling.

The pictures on the cards are seen as representative of people's problems and woes, their happiness and triumphs. Elements of the artwork are symbolic. Coins clearly signify money, wealth and prosperity. They have also come to mean the human body, the home and all things physical. The symbology of the tarot is a living thing that constantly evolves. In the distant past when people actually came into contact with pages, knights on horseback and were ruled by kings and queens, images of the same would have had a specific, visceral meaning. Nowadays, these same cards are viewed as allegories denoting the stages, ranks and levels of maturity in our lives.

Interpreting the Symbols

It is a hugely exciting time for tarot right now. Hundreds of beautiful decks are available on the mass market that have been created by tarot masters with great experience to address today's realities, while keeping faith with the symbols of the past. The Rock Art Tarot by Jerry Roelen, for example, is illustrated with prehistoric cave paintings and uses modern terminology, like Innocence for the Fool. The real key to understanding the tarot and getting the most out of it is to be open in your interpretation of the symbols. Any tarot reader can interpret the message of control and self-discipline that is integral to the Chariot card in the context of the question asked; but only you can realize that the ribbon tied around the charioteer's waist reminds you of the bow on a box of chocolates you ate in one go and made yourself sick from: a lesson in self-control. As people allow themselves more time for reflection these days, they are more apt to see themselves in all aspects of card art: as the horses dragging the burden, as the rider directing the horses, as the weighed-down cart, even as the reins transmitting instructions and emotions. The real beauty and wonder of the tarot is how intimate and personal its message is to each and every one of us.

The Classic Tarot

The tarot deck pictured throughout this book, published today by Lo Scarabeo as The Classic Tarot, was originally engraved in 1823 by the Milanese Carlo Dellarocca and is sometimes called the Soprafino deck. The artwork is similar to the oldest known deck, The Visconti (or Visconti Sforza) Tarot, painted in the mid-1400s. The Classic Tarot is especially beautiful, but there are many other decks available. The interpretations given in this book hold good whichever deck you choose.

Introduction

What is the Tarot?

The tarot has traditionally been used for divination, although some secret societies scoff at this and maintain the importance of other, more esoteric mystical uses. Recently, tarot has become recognized as a powerful tool for personal development and healing. Probably the most popular deck of modern times is the Rider-Waite deck, illuminated by the artwork of Pamela Coleman Smith and originally published by Rider in 1910. This was one of the first decks to show a fully illustrated minor arcana. Card numbers 1 to 10 were shown simply with repeated pictures of the suit symbol: one coin, two coins, three coins, and so on. The Classic Tarot illustrates this book.

Finding Solutions

Beginners often turn to the tarot when in a state of anxiety, when there's a problem with no obvious or easy answer: a lover has been cruel, bills are due, there's been an accident, morale is low at work. The tarot is certainly useful in working through such problems, although an advanced tarot reader will use the deck more proactively by planning ahead. Remember that you are reading this book because you are searching for positive change in your life. You are in touch with and trust your inner self. It is therefore vital that you work only with symbols and meanings that are positive and give you hope. Examine and meditate on every aspect of each card and create positive, encouraging definitions of the symbology. Frame your tarot questions in solution-generating terms. Define your tarot answers in life-affirming language.

Positive Energy

I've been asked again and again how the correct cards get dealt and why the same cards appear over and over. It's synchronicity. Everything comes together through the process of forming a question, shuffling the cards, laying them out and perceiving an answer. The universe really is alive and listening. When you express your desire as a wish or thought, you send energy outward. For every action, there is an equal and opposite reaction. Some form of energy comes back to you as a result of that wish or thought. Send out thoughts of how you will never find the right partner (a nice job, enough money) and, guess what, you won't. Send out thoughts that you WILL find the perfect lifemate (a fulfilling occupation, money in abundance), ask the tarot how, and you certainly will!

For many people, whose only knowledge of the tarot probably comes from sensationalist films, the tarot is something to be feared, especially when it comes to the 'dark' cards like Death and the Hanged Man. The truth of the matter is that death and sacrifice surround us in nature and are an integral part of daily life. The day dies as night is born. We sacrifice our time and energy to earn a living. Fear is caused by ignorance which can be cured by study of the tarot's 78 cards.

✝

The Journey of Everyman

We are all tasked with a journey at birth. We learn the goodness of family and fellowship, and we realize their temporality as we move out and away. We face temptation and experience disappointment and failure. We taste success and discover beauty and goodness, and eventually gain wisdom and knowledge. All these steps of Everyman's journey are illustrated in the archetypes of the tarot. We are all united by birth, growth, love and completion. We all embody struggle and lack, striving and want. Each symbol represents a universal truth that cuts through language barriers, cultural difference and political discord. You know better than anyone how the symbols relate to you and your life. You are Everyman, yet you are unique.

✝

Major and Minor Arcana

Life is a progression marked by accomplishments, from a baby's first step through to graduation day and beyond. Internal growth and progress can also be marked in stages. The numbered cards ('pips') of the minor arcana serve as markers of progress along four paths: willpower/instinctual, emotional/relational, mental/intellectual and physical/financial. These paths correspond to the dominant energy in the four suits, respectively Wands, Cups, Swords and Coins. The court cards, most commonly named Page, Knight, Queen and King, represent four ranks of achievement or maturity along each path.

The major arcana touch all of the high points, the crossroads of life, the major events. Beginning to end they illustrate the 'Hero's Journey' that we all find ourselves on. The peaks along the way are far higher than those symbolized by the minor arcana and the valleys much deeper. Many of the concepts and energies of the majors are found reflected in the minors, but as a softer echo. The Fool, for example, denotes the beginning of a major venture into the unknown, while the four aces of the minor arcana symbolize a less life-changing process in the area of the energy of each suit.

Reversals

Some tarot readers prefer not to use or interpret reversed (upside-down) cards, on the basis that there is already enough negativity in the world. Personally, I find that their use increases the communicative power of the tarot, so making it that much more useful as a tool for life planning.

A reversed card indicates something other than the same card seen upright, but not necessarily simply the opposite. Here are ten possible interpretations of a reversed card. The context given by the question asked - 'What do I need to do?', for example - will partly determine which shade of meaning applies. The specific spread or layout you are using, whether it's a Body/Mind/Spirit layout see pages 104-5), for example, will also have a bearing on which meaning you take from the reversed card's appearance. The third factor in the interpretation is the card's positional meaning; therefore a card in the physical, tangible Body position has a different resonance from a card in the ethereal, divine Spirit position.

POSSIBLE REVERSED MEANINGS

PROBLEM: Many people become interested in the tarot because they have problems. If the Ace of Coins appears in a reading, it may be that the questioner is approaching a new avenue of prosperity. Reversed, the Ace of Coins could mean there is a problem with this new prosperity.

OPPOSITE: If the Ace of Coins means a new avenue of prosperity, then the reversed Ace of Coins can mean the opposite: no new avenue of prosperity.

BLOCKED: A blocked reading indicates that the energy or meaning of the card is present but is blocked, so not fully present. Some effort is needed to bring it fully into play.

WEAKER: A reversed card may have the same meaning as the upright, only in a softer, weaker form.

LACK: It could be that the reversed card reveals a lack of what is shown by the upright. When this lack is addressed, things will proceed more favourably.

WARNING: Interpreted as a warning, a reversed card suggests that the current course of action is leading toward trouble or even danger.

DENIAL: It may be that the questioner is in denial about the upright meaning, as it applies to themselves or the situation in hand.

DELAY: The meaning of the upright card is being delayed for some reason. It will manifest itself eventually.

DECAY: The upright meaning is dwindling away. It cannot be counted on to remain.

CONTROLLED: The upright meaning is a problem that is currently under control. However, a reversed card indicates that its underlying causes have not been dealt with, and so it is likely to come back into play at any time.

Tarot Magick

Over the course of this book, I shall be showing you how to use tarot cards in many different ways: to perform basic readings for yourself and others; for tarot affirmations and meditations; in career counselling; to gain a deeper understanding of who you are and how you got here; to establish where you want to go and how best to go about it; to begin relationships and improve existing ones; to assist the healing process; even how to access the secrets of your genetic code.

Each card in the major arcana represents an energy that can be released – either to make that energy manifest in your life or, conversely, to make it disappear. If your wish is to invoke love in your life, for example, your task would be to release the energy symbolized by the Lovers card and willfully open yourself to love. To achieve the reverse – a banishment of the card's power from your life – you would burn, or otherwise destroy the card and willfully release that energy.

Spell Casting

Please remember that the spells of manifestation and banishment I shall be sharing with you are exactly that: spells. This isn't a primer on magick, and a basic working knowledge of how to prepare for spell casting is assumed. You are completely responsible for your actions and their reactions. I suggest you first create a sacred space by casting a protective circle. How you do this is up to you, and can be as simple as chanting the following:

> *Guardians of the East, Elementals of Air, Powers of Sight and Insight, be here now. Guardians of the South, Elementals of Fire, Powers of Passion and Strength, be here now. Guardians of the West, Elementals of Water, Powers of Healing and Feeling, be here now. Guardians of the North, Elementals of Earth, Powers of Stability and Prosperity, be here now.*

After casting, you need to stabilize yourself physically and mentally. These twin processes of grounding and centering, which most people achieve through meditation and deep breathing, will leave you calm, balanced and connected to your personal centre. Once you have released or destroyed the energy symbolized by the card you are working with, you can draw back your focus by reversing the process: releasing the circle, grounding and centering again. Release the circle with:

> *Guardians of the East, Elementals of Air, Powers of Sight and Insight, I release you. Guardians of the South, Elementals of Fire, Powers of Passion and Strength, I release you. Guardians of the West, Elementals of Water, Powers of Healing and Feeling, I release you. Guardians of the North, Elementals of Earth, Powers of Stability and Prosperity, I release you.*

Banishing Spells

When casting each spell, meditate on the card itself and picture exactly what you hope to accomplish. Keep that 'goal' firmly in mind as you create sacred space, ask for the help of your higher power, and light candles and herbs or perform whatever ritual you desire. For constructive spells, place the card where it can be viewed easily or place it under a fire-safe candleholder, to stay until the candle has burned down completely. For destructive spells, create a completely fire-safe place to burn the card, or bury it deep enough so that it won't work up with the rain. Ensure the process of release is complete: you don't want the card to carry a connection back your way later.

Visualizing Your Goals

For practical reasons, I highly recommend obtaining a duplicate deck. Some readers only use one deck their whole life, but this tends to prohibit the destructive spells. Banishing spells can be adjusted so as not to damage the card, but when I really have a strong desire to release something from my life, there is nothing like watching it go up in smoke! Take care because wax, ash, water, not to mention fire, can discolour or otherwise damage your cards. Be certain, too, that you really want to go ahead with the banishment. Are you sure you are done with that thing? Likewise when you call an energy into your life, be sure you truly want it.

chapter one
The Major Arcana

The real wonder of the tarot is the mystical journey of self-discovery it reveals: the path that takes us from stumbling Fool, through to the wise Hermit, and ultimately to the wholeness of the World. In this chapter, we will explore each of the major arcana one by one, looking at the divinatory meanings of the symbols and ways to interpret these in the context of modern life. For each, I have included an exercise to help you master the basics of tarot reading, as well as a Manifest/Banish section: using the card to change your life. Manifest means to invoke, create, grow or call that energy to you, while banish means to devoke, remove, destroy or send that energy away from you. Always be sure when working with these energies that you have crystal-clear intent. Without a clear goal, you can end up getting rid of the very thing you are trying to call to you, or strengthening the very thing you want to remove.

The Hero is a Fool

Where do our heroes come from? Where were they born? What did they eat? Where did they go to school? How do they support themselves? In reality, they all started out as the Fool. The Fool takes chances, leaps before he looks, and makes mistakes. Yet, through study and hard work, the Fool begins to master skills, gather knowledge and make some changes in his situation. He becomes the Magician. Then he delves inward as the High Priestess. What he finds on that inner journey is realized in the abundant fertility of the Empress. Now he who was once the Fool has something that means a lot to him. He must take care of it and be responsible for it, as the Emperor. He worries about how it looks to others, and accepts his place within society as the Hierophant (high priest). He discovers romantic companionship in the Lovers, and perhaps loses himself for a while. Control is regained with the Chariot.

The Fool Matures

Our Fool gains a sense of the reactions caused by his own actions in Justice. But it is his confusing, passionate experiences in Love and Justice that lead him to withdraw from society for a time and seek new and higher plateaus of wisdom as the Hermit. He gains insight into the endless, uncontrollable Wheel of Life in the Wheel of Fortune and determines to control his inner-self with Strength.

The Fool is a Hero

The Fool gives of himself as the Hanged Man and loses something forever in Death. He glimpses the beauty of immortality in Temperance, and has perhaps been tempered along his journey. He faces temptation in the Devil and tremendous upheaval in the Tower. These experiences lead to a new appreciation of his inner beauty, strength and wisdom in the Star. He struggles with one last illusion in the Moon and then emerges into the bright clarity of the Sun. At last he is ready for Judgement and steps into his own in the World. Are you ready to begin your Hero's Journey?

The Fool

The beginning of the journey

In classic tarot decks, this is the card that shows a young man stepping over a cliff while looking up at the sky. Often, a little dog is warning him in some way, but he is completely heedless.

And so the Fool denotes the beginning of a journey, task or relationship arrived at with little or no knowledge. Stepping out on the Fool's path takes courage of a kind that some might call reckless, but it also requires determination and independence. This card is about going your own way and dancing to your own inner music.

The Fool is the ultimate beginning, the spark of life that appears just after sperm and egg conjoin. The start of your physical body was the beginning of a new lifetime for your eternal spirit. This is the beginning of a stage, process or effort. It is the foolish choice to step off the ledge without looking; the child's choice to disregard their parents' wishes; the student's choice not to heed the teacher's advice and lessons. This is how new universes are discovered and conquered. The blessing of the Fool is the daring heroism that brings in an astonishing result against all the odds.

REVERSED MEANING

A blocked beginning | I have this great idea but I just can't manifest it | I don't have the money, the time, the energy, the will, the place, the car, the partner or whatever to make X happen. In other words, I simply don't want to start this thing | Tomfoolery to gain attention: I'm walking over the edge of a cliff solely because someone said I shouldn't.

APPEARANCE IN A SPREAD

The Fool appears to show you the path of daring, which is the only way to the heart's true desire. It tells you that it is good to dive right in and start following your dreams. How else will you make them happen?

USING THE CARD TO CHANGE YOUR LIFE

Each card in the major arcana can be used to make certain things manifest in – or disappear from – your life.

The Fool represents the wish to begin anew. Use the card whenever you plan to start a project or a new phase of your life. If you want to banish something from your life, use the card to dispel foolish behaviour, or to end a false beginning.

This exercise can be done with each card to help you learn it. Sit comfortably in a well-lit place with the Fool card before you and a notebook beside you. Calm and centre yourself. When you feel at peace:

- Look at the card and describe what you see.
- Look again and see what you left out: the colours and patterns, the background and the foreground. Look at the actions of the figures, imagine their thoughts and study their facial expressions.
- Think about the time of day and season of the year.
- What do these images and symbols mean to you? Think of an example from your personal experience.
- What else could the card mean? What else does it make you think of ?
- Everyone has their own set of beliefs, religious or otherwise. How does this card fit into your belief system? What does it mean when you place it in that context?
- Now turn the card upside down. Describe and define what you see, think and feel about it being reversed.
- What would this card in reverse imply in a reading?
- Decide on one or more keywords that bring all these associations back to you.

I The Magician

The power of the journey

The Magician is an alchemist of a forgotten age or a scientist of the modern one. He studies the nature of things, draws conclusions, and then makes changes to produce the desired results. The Magician symbolizes the power you have to exert your will on your present environment, to push against predestination. Taken one way, the Magician studies the way things work; from another perspective, he is the one that makes things work.

As Magicians, we use any tool that helps us. A tool can be any object – a good-luck charm, a writer's pen or computer, a teacher's blackboard – or something less tangible, like a personal characteristic or idea. The Magician enables us to channel energy into whatever tool is appropriate to effect the change we desire.

Be careful what you ask for because you may get it. Remember this and the cautionary tale of the sorcerer's apprentice, who overreached himself with disastrous consequences, whenever you perform magick or try to work change in your situation. Yes, you really do have the power, but do you know how to handle it? Are you ready for the consequences?

REVERSED MEANING

Effort that has backfired. My desire hasn't been achieved, or was achieved but wasn't what I wanted after all | I'm using the wrong tool for the job. I want a promotion, for example, and my chosen tool – be that assertiveness, deference, staying late, networking – is not getting me one | My effort was wrongly channelled. However, it isn't wasted: I can learn from this mistake and try again.

✛

Use the card to exert your inner will on an external situation, to make the change you desire. If you want to call back your will or change it in some way, use the card to perform a banishment.

The purpose of this exercise is to open up your psychic vision centre to your deck as a tool for self-guidance and positive change. You will need a purple candle and something to inscribe it – a toothpick or paring knife will do perfectly.

Purple is the colour of the third eye chakra (see pages 148–51), the area on the forehead between the eyes. This chakra is the centre of your psychic vision and intuition.

- Take your candle and inscribe it with your name and the name of your deck.
- Place the candle in an appropriate fire-safe holder behind your deck.
- Concentrate your mind fully on the purpose of the exercise.
- Light the candle and rest your hand on your deck.
- Gaze into the flame and let thoughts about the deck, and tarot reading in general, run through your mind.
- Look at the deck card by card.
- Shuffle your deck as long as is comfortable.
- Let the candle burn out, or extinguish it so you can use it again for this exercise at another time.

APPEARANCE IN A SPREAD

The Magician points to your ability to make a small change in one thing and thereby effect change on a grander scale. Changing the perceptions of those around you is impressive magick, but consider shifting your own perceptions first. Think seriously about the ramifications of any change.

✛

2 The High Priestess

The inner journey

The High Priestess is about studying the wisdom within. This card is also about accepting the will of outside events and letting things be. The Priestess sees beyond the veil of tangible reality, into the mysterious darkness of creation and existence. She teaches us the value of striving to understand and work in harmony with forces that already are. Her message is to know and accept your inner self. Go with the flow. Listen to your heart and mind, accept the bad as well as the good, take the rough with the smooth: they exist hand in hand within nature.

This is a powerfully feminine card, perhaps reflecting the way that women more easily and fully appreciate the mysteries of nature and life. Whereas women tend to be able to see beyond the material appearance of things, men traditionally view the world in more rational terms. This card encourages us all to put rational thinking aside for a time, to seek esoteric knowledge and explore our possibilities on an internal, subtle and spiritual plane.

REVERSED MEANING

I'm not seeing the situation for what it is because I'm concentrating on the outward, obvious appearance of things | Take a walk on the wild side | It's time to embrace the feminine side of my self | I need to trust my intuition and stop denying intangible evidence.

APPEARANCE
IN A SPREAD

Modern spiritualists speak of the Akashic records, the records of all knowledge. Biologists speak of genetic memory. We all carry certain truths and knowledge within ourselves. The appearance of the High Priestess is our impetus to begin the search for this knowledge. She gives us the confidence that ancient truths, wisdom, ancestral memories and esoteric mysteries are there for us to find.

USING THE CARD TO CHANGE YOUR LIFE

Call the energy of the High Priestess to begin the search for your own inner mysteries and truths. Release the High Priestess to dispel something you are not yet ready for or able to deal with. Sometimes the truth is too harsh or disturbing, or comes at an inappropriate time, and you need to shut down the channel.

Dream your way to better, more powerful tarot interpretation by practising the following exercise:

- Take pen and paper and make a list of everything you desire to accomplish with your tarot deck. For example:

  'I want to ... understand myself better;

  ... help others to understand themselves better;

  ... learn the rich history and culture of tarot;

  ... become a paid reader.'

  Include some negatives in your list as well, like 'I don't want to be a two-dimensional person' or 'I don't want to be in any way ostracized because of my tarot reading.'

- Put the list under your pillow when you go to bed. When you wake in the morning, burn the list in a flame and release your desires to the universe.

3 The Empress

The conception of the journey

The Empress resides in the realm of clean living, blooming with health and fertility. Some see the Empress as the fruitful union of the Magician and High Priestess. She symbolizes both the worldly success of the harvest and also the conception within, that must be nurtured and birthed. She is grounded and centred, stable and supporting. To discover the Empress, think flowers, plants and gardening; think springtime, a time to gestate something in your life and help it grow.

The Empress is a ruler, superior to all queens, yet she is down to earth, and concerned for the land and her people. Despite her status, she actually owns very little in her own name. All that she has is the property of her people. Her message is to be happy with what you have. Take notice of the abundance that is yours. Cherish it; nurture it and allow it to nurture and support you. Meditate on the real meaning of abundance: what it means to have everything you need, and be truly and fully satisfied. Learn to let go of the illusion that your wants are denied.

REVERSED MEANING

✠ A blocked or stunted development | I'm having trouble concentrating on a project right through to the end | I'm not appreciating all that I have. ✠

APPEARANCE
IN A SPREAD

This card reminds you that you have all that is needed for health, happiness, love and success – within you. While there's no point denying it would be fun to win the lottery and be rich beyond our wildest dreams, most of us in the West have more than enough already. We all know that wealth in the material sense doesn't necessarily make people happy. The Empress concerns herself with abundance of a more spiritual nature. True contentment comes from within.

USING THE CARD TO CHANGE YOUR LIFE

The Empress represents new life. Manifest her energy to gestate an idea or project, then give birth to it. Banish the Empress to slow down or halt the growth of something that is happening too fast in your life.

This exercise uses a concept known as 'modelling', otherwise known as 'fake it till you make it'. The first step to becoming a certain kind of person is to start acting as though you already are that person. Only time separates you from the desired result. Try this exercise with any card that holds the energy you want to model in your life.

- Go through your deck and pull out the Empress card.
- Make a list in your tarot journal of what the Empress is doing, wearing, where she is, even what she is thinking. In some decks she is pregnant and gardening, spinning wool, or simply enthroned and imperious. In our Classic deck, she has a tight bodice and holds a staff of office, and a shield with an eagle on it. Her crown looks heavy with gold, rubies, emeralds and sapphires. She gazes out regally and with beneficence upon her subjects.
- Consider what props you have at your disposal that you can use to emulate the Empress. Perhaps you can make a staff using a stick of some sort and a big red piece of costume jewellery, or you could transform your favourite chair into a throne.
- Assume the mantle of the Empress by wearing her colours and adding an eagle brooch, or anything that helps you to feel like her.
- Crown yourself the ruler of your own destiny.
- Tell yourself that you deserve abundance in all things because you are worthy. You are an extraordinary human being and you deserve no less than the very best.

The Emperor

The authority of the journey

The Emperor is the king of kings, the supreme ruler or ultimate authority. Almost always represented as male, he exhibits traditionally masculine qualities of leadership, aggressiveness, decisiveness and responsibility. He is held accountable for what goes on within his court and also for the conduct of his imperial citizens abroad. The Emperor has many advisers but the final say is his alone. As befits his status, he is granted all luxury and facility. It's his responsibility to use these gifts in the service of his office, and not to abuse his privilege.

In some societies, the Emperor was a figure equated with God. In others, he was the representative of God on Earth, or else just an extremely smart, powerful, lucky man. This card is primarily about personal authority and responsibility.

The Emperor has to control his own life before he can rule over anyone else. We decide, daily, whether to be the Emperor and take control, whether to rule our empire according to a godly or secular standard, or to refuse the position and let things happen as they will. Who is the Emperor of your life?

REVERSED MEANING

I have a problem related to authority, whether that means management at work, the government or red tape | Any authority I have is in name only; it isn't real or respected | No one is taking responsibility and it's having a negative effect | I find it hard to make this decision.

USING THE CARD TO CHANGE YOUR LIFE

The Emperor is a symbol of power and the responsibility that comes with it. Manifest his energy in order to accept your own authority and influence over yourself, other people and situations. Banish the Emperor when you need to relinquish your hold on something or someone.

One of the most frustrating things about life is that we can't make other people act in the way that we feel is right. The following exercise helps you explore and define how to work with other people, and how to put your foot down when necessary. You can adapt it to cover any type of relationship or situation.

Go through the deck and pull out the Emperor card. Place it above your workspace so that you can see him easily. He will remind you to think in terms of exerting your authority.

Shuffle the rest of the deck as you consider the following three questions and then pull out three cards to answer them.

- **CARD 1** What kind of authority do I have over this person (relationship, situation, etc.)?
- **CARD 2** What blocks my authority?
- **CARD 3** How can I exert my authority?

EXAMPLE READING

CARD 1 12 THE HANGED MAN: The authority I have over this person is due to the sacrifices I have made for them. Perhaps it is asking too much to expect them to reciprocate and sacrifice things for me, or to appreciate the sacrifices I have made for them. | **CARD 2** 6 THE LOVERS: My weakness in this situation is love, which is blocking my authority. Yet it was my choice to enter into this relationship and to make sacrifices. I can choose to leave the relationship. | **CARD 3** 10 THE WHEEL OF FORTUNE: This card tells us to make our own luck. In this reading, its appearance advises me to wait for the most fortunate circumstance, when my lover seems receptive, to exert my authority and ask that they change their behaviour.

APPEARANCE IN A SPREAD

When I met the eminent psychologist and philosopher Timothy Leary in 1983, he had changed his original slogan of 'Turn on, tune in and drop out!' to 'Tune in, turn on, take charge!' The Emperor's appearance is a reminder that we each have ultimate power over our own life. You deserve the riches that are yours. Claim them and use them for the greatest good. Be the benevolent dictator in your own life.

5 The Hierophant

The observer of the journey

All societies, traditions and cultures have a guiding authority in addition to a governing authority, be it a priest, shaman or philosopher. The Hierophant guides behaviour that doesn't necessarily fall under the law, usually pertaining to morality and matters that are perceived as good for society at large. He represents an external conscience: the all-seeing eye of society that controls the actions of individuals. This is about letting the opinion of others guide your behaviour, regardless of whether this tallies with your personal sense of right and wrong.

The Hierophant compares easily to Big Brother in the political or social arena.

Whereas the High Priestess represents true divinity, the Hierophant, or High Priest, symbolizes secular religion. It's the difference between experiencing a tangible relationship with the Goddess (or any deity) and showing up for church on Sunday, the latter being a good example of form without content. The difference between the Hierophant and the Emperor, to compare it another way, is the difference between church and state.

REVERSED MEANING

I am merely seeking approval, not genuine knowledge | People aren't going to understand my action or choice | I am one of society's outcasts, and as such have a unique perspective. I can choose to embrace this position or conform.

APPEARANCE
IN A SPREAD

The Hierophant tends to make an appearance when the querent is considering doing something unconventional. While the 10 of Cups card represents the emotions and the nitty gritty of a successful, happy long-term relationship, the Hierophant is more interested in buying the white dress and exchanging vows and rings in front of a crowd. That's not such a bad thing. Social convention, traditions and the rules they generate do a lot of good in society. But always living by the rules can kill the spirit of the individual.

USING THE CARD TO CHANGE YOUR LIFE

The Hierophant wields his power for good or ill. He can be any leader who controls the actions and decisions of others. Manifest the Hierophant to invoke an understanding of your place within society. Burn this card in sacred space when you leave the service of an oppressive leader, or to banish Big Brother's influence on your behaviour.

A one-card daily draw is very popular among tarot readers and extremely useful as a learning tool. As with any reading, start by calming and centring yourself and clearly establishing your intent.

- Think about what you really want to know and how best to express it as a question.
- Shuffle and cut the deck as you like and draw one card to answer your question.
- Look at it, meditate on it, and think about it throughout the day.
- Note your realizations in your tarot journal.

EXAMPLE READING

The following questions are answered as though the card drawn in the daily draw is the Hierophant.

WHAT IS THE MOST IMPORTANT THING FOR ME TO DO TODAY? To be open to acting as an official of some kind, and to be wary of someone wanting a 'rubber stamp' of approval for their actions. | **WHAT IS THE MOST IMPORTANT THING FOR ME TO REALIZE TODAY?** That I desire the approval of friends and society, and sometimes I may act in a way contrary to my nature in order to gain that approval. | **WHAT CAN I LEARN TODAY?** Today is a good day to compare the external and internal conscience, to question how I would react to any given circumstance if no one was watching. | **WHAT DOES THE UNIVERSE WANT FROM ME TODAY?** To be circumspect in my behaviour, and seriously consider how my words and actions affect others.

𝔅 The Lovers

The choice of the journey

Love is a divine gift, the ultimate pleasure, and the goal of so much effort. Being struck by Cupid makes one so giddy and light, it is often described as a spiritual feeling. The experience is uplifting and not of this world. Love brings happiness and joy of a kind that can even heal physical illness. Nearly all the songs ever written are about love, whether romantic love, devotion to God, the love of parents for their children, the love between comrades in arms, or the love one has for one's country.

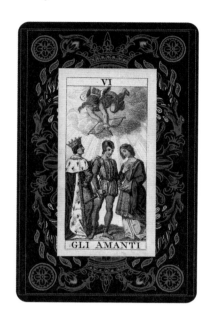

The Lovers card is all about choice. It's an exciting draw and summons up idealized visions of perfect romantic union. Yet how many of us have made foolish choices based on infatuation and lust? How often is love credited with causing pain? This card embraces all the different levels of love and lust and asks us to make the choice between them. Do you want instant gratification or do you want long-term security? What are you willing to give in order to get what you want? These are decisions only you can make, and actions only you can take.

You must first love yourself, then you can love the world.

REVERSED MEANING

Lust is masquerading as love | There is infidelity and dishonesty in the air | I need to rethink my choice in the situation under question. (In this case, the card is interpreted more generally, and my choice needn't be specifically related to love.) | Now is not the best time for a whirlwind romance.

APPEARANCE
IN A SPREAD

This card most often appears when what the querent really needs to do is learn to love themselves, but instead feels desperate to find the right partner. Only when we truly love ourselves can we accept that we deserve to be loved by someone of worth.

USING THE CARD TO CHANGE YOUR LIFE

Affirm the Lovers card in your daily life to call love in all its forms into your life and into your heart. That's self-esteem, affection in all your relationships, and devotion to your higher power. Deny the Lovers card to banish silly lusts or infatuations from your life; banish all shallow admiration, inappropriate sentimentality and embarrassing crushes.

The three-card spread is probably the most popular of the tarot readings and the most often practised. It's wonderfully versatile as it opens up three viewpoints on any one issue, or gives a glimpse of three different issues, or brings light to two issues and throws up a third new idea. Ask yourself three pertinent questions, such as:

- **CARD 1** What's the state of my love life?
- **CARD 2** What's blocking my love life?
- **CARD 3** What can help my love life?

EXAMPLE READING

CARD 1 1 THE MAGICIAN (REVERSED): Blocked manifestation; my love life is not happening in the way that it could. Things could be better and I could be more fulfilled | **CARD 2** 3 THE EMPRESS: The abundance symbolized by the Empress suggests I don't feel any need or lack, and that's why I'm not putting enough effort into my love life | **CARD 3** 2 THE HIGH PRIESTESS (REVERSED): The High Priestess appears reversed to tell me my love life would improve if I blocked my esoteric pursuits. Sounds simple, and yet esoteric pursuits are the love of my life.

7 The Chariot

The vehicle of the journey

The energy of the Chariot is that of learned discipline and self-control. It pertains to the lessons and behaviour we learn through habit and from fear of punishment or negative consequences. It's a discipline that is imposed from outside, like military training, or the strength and self-control that comes from correcting your own mistakes. You are the one steering the Chariot, deciding where it goes and how fast.

Pay attention to the road ahead; don't get lost gazing out of the window at the countryside. The Charioteer is not one to be distracted. He is focused upon his destination.

Discipline is required for your spiritual journey, too. Tarot readings have many layers of meaning, all of which are simultaneously true. The Chariot is a reminder to stay on course during your spiritual journey as well as in the journey of your physical life. Some spiritual truths can only be learned through the hard knocks of life. Just like any physical discipline, spiritual self-control is learned through experience.

REVERSED MEANING

The self-control I'm exerting is inappropriate given the situation | I've lost control. I'm being driven by circumstance and it's time to take the reins again | Loss of focus and direction; I need to remind myself of where I'm heading. What's my ultimate goal?

APPEARANCE IN A SPREAD

The Chariot can be a warning that you are driving yourself too hard. On a more literal level, it can also indicate road driving. The card often appears when the questioner is going to be doing more driving than normal, or is involved in a long-distance romance or has a long journey to work.

USING THE CARD TO CHANGE YOUR LIFE

Manifest the Chariot to bring yourself improved self-discipline and self-control when embarking on a new weight-loss programme, exercise regime or gruelling schedule. Banish the Chariot to shed senseless, rigid or unproductive habits. You may be obsessed about perfecting your hair before going to work in the morning, but would it be such a disaster if you didn't?

The 'clarification card' enables you to look further below the surface for an alternative meaning, when the outward appearance of things doesn't make sense or doesn't tell the whole story. It is used in this two-card exercise to provide more information and to reveal hidden meaning.

Ask yourself a question. Draw a card for a direct answer, and a second card for clarification:

- **CARD 1** What is the best use of my time today?
- **CARD 2** Why?

EXAMPLE READING

CARD 1 7 THE CHARIOT: I'm going to drive into town to have lunch with my friend, but maintain the self-discipline to drive back to work afterwards. | **CARD 2** 2 THE HIGH PRIESTESS: The Priestess appears to tell me to look within, beyond the superficiality of reason and rationalization. Her energy can be quite irrational. The truth is I just wanted to skip work and go shopping! This second card underlines my need to exert the self-control of the Chariot today.

8 Justice

The responsibility of the journey

The Justice card represents the necessity of taking responsibility for your decisions and actions. Realize two things about Justice as you familiarize yourself with the card. One, you are responsible for the consequences of your actions. Two, what goes around comes around; if you want something to happen, you're going to have to act. People who pray for justice don't have any knowledge of the ancient Vedic laws of karma – for every action, there is an equal and opposite reaction. Imagine if you had to die for every animal that died for your food. That's karma and that would be true justice, of a kind that is automatically carried out by nature.

Within society, Justice is one of our highest ideals. Justice demands that we seek fairness on behalf of all citizens, recompense victims, punish evil-doers and protect the community at large from their actions. Yet this earthly Justice is dispensed by humans who are imperfect and make mistakes, sometimes compounding the very injustices they seek to redress. The balance of perfect Justice represents the ideal. The double-edged sword she holds is the reality.

REVERSED MEANING

I am acting irresponsibly and I'm ignoring the consequences of my actions | There is a lack of justice in the given situation | Something illegal is going on | Life's just not fair sometimes.

APPEARANCE IN A SPREAD

The Justice card often appears as a positive indicator in a law-related issue, suggesting a favourable judgement or a helpful continuation in a legal case. This card may also be pointing out the relationship between cause and effect.

USING THE CARD TO CHANGE YOUR LIFE

Use Justice purposefully to accept responsibility for your actions. Destroy the Justice card to banish or minimize the effects of a wrongful legal decision.

This four-card draw is an excellent way to take an impartial snapshot of the state of your relationship.

- **CARD 1** What is the present state of the relationship?
- **CARD 2** What is my situation or position?
- **CARD 3** What is my partner's situation or position?
- **CARD 4** How should I proceed?

EXAMPLE READING

A year or so ago, a friend came to see me who had recently started a new relationship. This was the first serious relationship she had ever had and she was feeling very uncertain. I carried out the four-card relationship reading to help her assess her emotions and view her situation positively, without fear.

CARD 1 0 THE FOOL: For my friend, this relationship was a brand-new beginning, with endless possibilities and an uncertain outcome. She felt that she had taken that Fool's step off the cliff and could hit rock bottom at any time. | **CARD 2** 2 THE HIGH PRIESTESS: My friend's situation was described by the High Priestess. She is an intuitive reader and active pagan. Her new partner, on the other hand, was not spiritual in any way. | **CARD 3** 4 THE EMPEROR: My friend found it interesting that the Emperor had been drawn to represent her partner as it was the card she had been actively manifesting in her life that year. She told me her partner was very much in control of their life and took responsibility for their choices and actions. They may also have been assuming authority in their relationship. | **CARD 4** 8 JUSTICE: The Justice card in answer to the final question communicated that, if my friend wanted to have some impact in this relationship, she needed to take action, rather than remain a passive partner.

9 The Hermit

The light of the journey

The Fool is now the wise old man who lives in a hermitage atop a high mountain. He has gained this lofty position by passing through all the archetypes shown in previous cards. By this stage in the journey, he has renounced his rule of the empire and gone beyond justice and the need for strict self-control.

Climb the mountain and seek wisdom and peace. Withdraw from your regular activities and social life for a little while. Give yourself time to assimilate past experiences. Let the light of the Lamp of Knowledge illuminate your heart and mind. Do whatever is necessary to create a space where you can seek answers to the question of your life's purpose. Some people are natural introverts. This isn't a fault or problem that needs correction. Honour the introvert that is the Hermit and discover his strengths. Spend some time out in nature or in solitude. Listen to silence. Slow down and be observant of the universe's natural cycles, then check in with your own natural bodily and mental cycles. Disconnect. Retreat. Seek wisdom within. Do some candle or crystal gazing and you will feel the benefits.

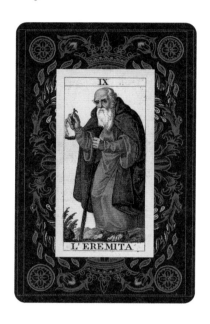

REVERSED MEANING

Something or someone is blocking my retreat | The Lamp of Knowledge is burning me because I have learned something I didn't want to know | I'm going in the wrong direction or looking in the wrong place for what I seek | Although it's a good idea to withdraw from some things, that doesn't mean I should retreat from everything.

APPEARANCE
IN A SPREAD

The Hermit appears to give you the power to light your own path through life. You don't need the help or guidance of others; their path is not yours and what is right for them isn't necessarily right for you. You must discover your very own path to wisdom.

USING THE CARD TO CHANGE YOUR LIFE

Manifest the Hermit to allow yourself to withdraw from your normal activities. Turn off your devices and do whatever it takes to find some free space. Banish the Hermit to end an extended period of introspection or loneliness.

Confirmation cards are a very useful tool in tarot reading. This exercise enables you to explore possible answers to your question before shuffling the deck and drawing the cards, which then act as confirmation.

- Think about what you need to get done today and make a list. Perhaps you need to get some exercise or do some chores round the house.

- Now ask the tarot 'What activities are best for me to focus on today?'

- Shuffle the deck and choose as many cards as you have options on your list. The first card will tell you what is the most important thing for you to focus on today, by confirming one item on the list. The last card will confirm which item is the least important.

- If the cards you pick don't confirm any of the activities on your list, open your mind to new ideas.

EXAMPLE READING

MEDITATION 9 THE HERMIT: The Hermit tells me to turn my focus inward and seek inner wisdom. | **EXERCISE** 7 THE CHARIOT: Symbolizing self-control achieved through practice and self-discipline, the Chariot supports the notion of taking care of myself physically, like a well-trained chariot horse or well-oiled chariot wheel. | **GARDENING** 3 THE EMPRESS: The abundance represented by the Empress is the perfect endorsement of working with nature. | **HOBBY** 17 THE STAR: This card tells me to follow my muse. As such it would support any plans I have to pursue whatever I find inspirational.

The Wheel of Fortune

The luck of the journey

Up and down, round and round, life keeps going on and on. The symbol of a spinning wheel is present in many cultures. In ancient India the samsara representation of karma – a spoked wheel that you often see on temples – symbolizes the endless chain of action and reaction, birth and death and rebirth. Chakras, represented by coloured circles or spheres, denote the metaphysical energy of the body, mind and soul. Symbolic of the eternal cycle, the wheel reminds us of the continuous flow of life that takes us from birth through growth, fruition, decay, death and rebirth; from spring through the seasons of the year; from sunrise through the times of the day. It denotes your cycle of rising in the morning, your daytime activities, your rest at night; and the cyclic lessons of your personal, professional and spiritual lives.

In the West we are trained to think linearly. When we see a wheel, we imagine it rolling backward or forward down a narrow road. In the East, the wheel of one's life is more like a sphere, and any direction is possible at any time. Now is a time of infinite possibility. Push the wheel of your life in the direction you want it to go.

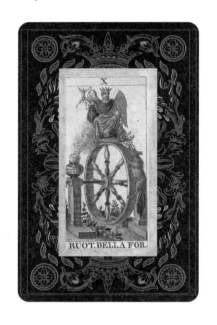

REVERSED MEANING

There is something blocking my good fortune. It's not my lucky day | I've reached the bottom or declining side of a cycle; things are drawing to a close | I need to prepare for winter or a time of lack | It's time for a new direction in some part of my life.

USING THE CARD TO CHANGE YOUR LIFE

Use the Wheel of Fortune card to bring yourself knowledge of the most favourable circumstances for your project or idea. Banish the Wheel of Fortune to dispense with bad luck or counteract ill omens.

Try this lucky charm exercise whenever it seems you've had a string of bad luck and things aren't going your way, whether it's your love life that's suffering, work is difficult, or you keep on stubbing your toe.

- Ask the tarot what three things you can do today to increase your luck.
- Shuffle your deck and pick three cards. Use these to perform the three charms.

APPEARANCE IN A SPREAD

If the Wheel of Fortune is drawn, pay attention to opportunity and take advantage of it. It's a message to turn a little gain into a big achievement. Anything can happen. Today is your lucky day; make the most of it!

CHARM 1 Examine your three cards. If you get upright cards, it means 'do this'. Reversed cards mean 'stop doing this'. | **CHARM 2** Notice the symbols and colours present in the three cards. Consider what they mean to you. Several cards in the Wands suit could mean that you need to get out your own 'magic wand' and exert your willpower. A preponderance of one colour could be read as a hint to light a candle and work with the corresponding chakra (see pages 148–51). | **CHARM 3** Wrap the three cards in a cloth or bag and carry them with you to ward off bad luck throughout the day. Keep looking at them to discover their full message.

Strength

The trial of the journey

The struggle of life makes us stronger. In some tarot decks, the human figure pictured in the Strength card is shown grappling with a lion (or other formidable beast); in others, she is gently leading him. In any case, considerable effort and strength have been exerted to achieve the final outcome – a controlled and therefore safe lion. This archetype is about inner strength and control. In truth, it's a sign of weakness to beat something into submission; it takes a much greater and more subtle strength to work out an equitable compromise.

True strength is found in personal honour and integrity. No matter how weak you are physically, you can emulate the archetype by exhibiting strength of character, strength of conviction, endurance, tolerance and tenacity in your life. The strength of love is a force that moves mountains. Acquire this strength by nurturing all you hold dear, maintain your relationships by giving positive encouragement, and embody the values championed by the lion tamer.

REVERSED MEANING

My inner strength and ability to endure is underdeveloped | Hell hath no fury like that of a person scorned. Someone is heading for serious trouble | Strength is being used for a wrong purpose or against the wrong person | It's time for some tough love.

APPEARANCE
IN A SPREAD

The Strength card is a reminder to continue on a positive path, no matter how hard it is. Showing consistent love and kindness in your dealings with children, vulnerable people and animals is the key to getting the best results in the long term, even if you are knocked back in the process. You catch more kittens with sardines than vinegar.

USING THE CARD TO CHANGE YOUR LIFE

Draw on the power of the Strength card to invoke physical, mental or spiritual endurance. This is the force to call upon when marshalling your resources for physical or mental battle. Banish Strength to dispel weakness or rigidity of any kind, whether that means emotional cowardice or a stiff neck.

Use the following visualization to boost your energies in the area of Strength. Begin by finding somewhere peaceful, where you won't be disturbed. Place the Strength card in front of you. When you are sitting comfortably, breathe deeply until you feel centred in yourself and grounded in existence.

- Close your eyes and imagine your favourite mountain. Consider the nature of the mountain: how vast and strong it is, how it supports all the trees, animals and even houses that reside on it.

- Connect your spirit to the mountain. Feel the strength and energy of the mountain flowing into you. Let the force of the mountain fill you with strength, conviction and endless endurance.

- When you are full to overflowing with strength, thank the mountain and disconnect.

- Let your consciousness bring you back to the room. Let any excess energy sink down into the earth beneath you.

- Open your eyes and programme the Strength card to serve as your visual focus from now on. It will function as a key that unlocks the endless strength of the mountain within you.

- Reinforce your sense of inner strength whenever necessary by returning to the Strength card.

The Hanged Man

The sacrifice of the journey

The Hanged Man hangs not from his neck, but upside down, from one foot. Although he isn't comfortable in this position, he isn't in any real danger either. Within the tarot milieu, he serves as a representation of sacrifice, whether for the good of others or for some future benefit. This experience can be compared to holding your breath as you dive for precious pearls. You may feel upside down, as though your hands are tied and that you are acting contrary to your nature, but this state of being will help someone else in some way, or even yourself in the future.

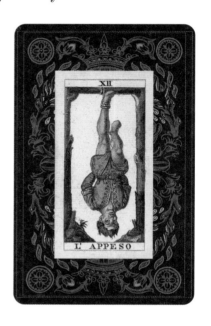

The Hanged Man may demand a drastic change in perspective. The mountain you face shrinks to a mere molehill when viewed as a step toward your cherished goal. Let the obstacles become challenges. Let the difficulties you experience in the act of sacrifice build your character. This card deals with the long term and the bigger picture. It's about seeing the wider truth and going beyond petty arguments of positive/negative, right/wrong or mine/yours. Remember that true sacrifice is made with no hope or desire of gain.

REVERSED MEANING

I'm holding back in some way | I need to give less of myself because my position has become untenable | I shouldn't be taking credit for doing something I wanted to do or was going to do anyway | Suffering is being confused with sacrifice.

APPEARANCE
IN A SPREAD

The appearance of the Hanged Man indicates that some sort of sacrifice is necessary, whether of time, energy, money or some other valuable commodity. The sacrifice should be made even though there is no guarantee that the desired result will be achieved.

USING THE CARD TO CHANGE YOUR LIFE

Release the energies of the Hanged Man to clarify exactly what kind of sacrifice is needed to help your situation. Banish his energies to be rid of unnecessary or artificial sacrifice. It can be tempting to take up a pose of martyrdom for appearance's sake.

Finding the will to make sacrifices is often a case of drawing back and seeing things in another way. The reading below allows you to practise this.

EXAMPLE READING

In this example reading, the Hanged Man card is placed in the middle of the table and two cards are placed on either side of him. The four cards are read twice. On first reading, cards 1 and 2 relate to how I am feeling about my relationship, and cards 3 and 4 explain how my partner is feeling. The energy of the Hanged Man is then harnessed in order to turn the viewpoint upside down, so that cards 1 and 2 represent my partner's point of view and cards 3 and 4 represent mine. Below is an example of how certain cards may be interpreted for the first reading. For the second reading, apply their meaning to your partner instead.

CARD 1 7 of Coins (reversed): This card suggests blocked patience. Perhaps I am feeling impatient with my partner but am unable to express my irritation. | **CARD 2** 7 of Wands (reversed): The second description of my relationship is blocked defiance. I need to find a calm time to sit down with my partner and talk through any disagreements. | **CARD 3** 8 of Coins (reversed): As a symbol of blocked mastery, this card tells me that my partner feels unable to control something in the relationship. | **CARD 4** 10 of Cups: This positive card, representing success, reassures me that my partner considers this relationship very successful.

13 Death

The end of the journey?

Everything in the material world is temporary and eventually comes to an end. Why is this so terrifying? If you become aware of your eternal spiritual nature, all need for fear is removed. In the West we are encouraged to develop linear, begining-to-end thought processes, whereby Death represents the absolute end of everything. You'd think that the Death card would be the last of the major arcana. It isn't because Death is merely a spoke on the wheel of life, the gate to the afterlife. It's a step in a process, a stage in development. The body dies but the spirit remains.

In tarot readings, the Death card tells us that it is time to bring things to a close – to shut a business or project down, to end a relationship, to cut whatever ties that bind us so we can clear away the old and unused and make room for the new. When Death appears, it's time to scythe your final harvest and reap what you have sown. Sweep away the junk and close that chapter of your life.

Death often reminds us of those who have gone before. Many cultures include a Day of the Dead or Memorial Day in their annual calendar to honour the dead.

REVERSED MEANING

The end is near but it isn't here yet | I'm not ready to say goodbye to this job, house, relationship, project or whatever it is I'm involved in. Why is this? | I'm cutting off or ending the wrong thing | I'm gathering life clutter when I should be discarding it.

APPEARANCE
IN A SPREAD

Death tells you to face the fact that the flesh of the situation is rotted away and gone. The bones or framework remain, however, and can be built upon later.

USING THE CARD TO CHANGE YOUR LIFE

The Death card is wonderfully useful as a tool for closure. Manifest its power to help you end a phase that is no longer of benefit to you. Banish Death to be rid of the 'ending energy' in a situation that still demands your attention.

I call this exercise 'Lucky 13'. Use it to confront an ending that was/is painful for you. Take pen and paper and find yourself a calm, quiet, safe and sacred space. A scented pink, green or white candle will help you see the negatives in a positive light.

- Giving yourself plenty of time, realize 13 lessons you have learned from this painful experience. Consider what insights you have gained, and what qualities you cherish in yourself now because of the experience.
- Write down your 13 realizations so that you can look back to them when painful memories surface.
- Use your list as armour in your future journey, and as a reminder of how to avoid such pain in the future. By remembering the 13 lessons, you prove to the universe and to yourself that you have learned them and never need to repeat them.

14 Temperance

The balance of the journey

When the Fool dies, his journey continues with either the angel pictured in Temperance or the Devil, which is our next card, or else he resides with both. In almost all decks, Temperance is depicted by a heavenly being who pours the nectar of immortality, or water of life (depending on your perspective) from one vessel into another. Just so, the eternal spirit moves from body to body through the process of reincarnation. The cycle of life continues, energy is conserved and balance maintained.

In daily life, balance translates as moderation. Temperance can be defined as equanimity and even-handedness. Bring your life into balance by acting with forethought and keeping an even temper. It sounds easy enough when you're calm, but we all know what a challenge it can be when the going gets tough.

Temperance can also refer to tempering the steel of your soul. A blade becomes strong and supple by being repeatedly stuck in a hot fire and hammered against an anvil. Remember temperance when it feels as though your life is in flames and your only alternative is the frying pan. It's your chance to become hard as steel.

REVERSED MEANING

I'm all out of balance and need to regain some equilibrium | This is like time going backwards or water flowing uphill | I've lost objectivity along with my temper | I need to moderate my behaviour and curb excess.

APPEARANCE
IN A SPREAD

Temperance appears to remind you of the importance of a balanced perspective. Seek balance in all aspects of your life, and restructure imbalance by adding or subtracting something to bring the situation into balance – whether that means spending less or more time with your partner, adding meditation to your daily routine or cutting down on hours spent in the office.

Manifest Temperance to imbue your body with vitality. Balance and moderation in your life give you energy, whereas excess leads to exhaustion. Banish Temperance to reverse the normal flow of time.

This exercise gives you the space to analyze and plan any changes you wish to make to areas of your life that have become dysfunctional.

- Pick an issue or area in your life that you feel is out of balance, then go through your deck and find a card that best describes it.

- Meditate on this card and the identified imbalance.

- Identify the counterbalance needed to correct the imbalance, then go through your deck and find a card that best describes this.

- Place your two cards upright and back-to-back on a flat surface, so that they balance without your help. You'll need a surface with friction, like a cloth, so that the cards don't slide.

- Repeat the meditation each time you set them up; they probably won't stand for long. As you gain expertise in balancing these cards, you will improve your ability to bring balance to your situation.

- Add more card couples that denote energies you feel need balancing in your life. Build a card house!

The Devil

15

The temptation of the journey

Some people believe in the Devil as an actual being who is opposed to the goodness of God; others use the term more figuratively, describing evil acts as the 'devil's work'. Whether he's a nemesis on your life's journey or a bogey-man used to manipulate the inner child, the Devil embodies a warning to be careful. Watch out for danger, whether physical, mental or spiritual.

People adopt self-destructive behaviour for seemingly incomprehensible reasons. You watch friends shoot themselves in the foot over and over again. It seems obvious, yet they haven't a clue. Or they escape their problems with drink and drugs, and then profess bewilderment that their problems have grown worse. This is the most prevalent energy of the Devil – doing the exact opposite of what is needed to achieve your desires.

The Devil promotes ignorance of one's true nature. You consider yourself someone with needs, wants, possessions and qualities, when in reality you are pure spirit with no needs, wants or possessions at all. Your natural state is to be happy and full of wisdom, not miserable and smothered by material worries.

REVERSED MEANING

There is no evil in this situation, although it may not seem that way | I have the power to avert danger if I act now | I have time and the will to avoid self-destruction. I am not obliged to continue on this negative path | I'm not tempted so there's no real danger.

APPEARANCE IN A SPREAD

The Devil makes himself known to warn you that temptation awaits. There is a high likelihood that the course you are on, or the action you are considering, will lead to self-destruction. Reconsider your plans in order to avoid danger.

USING THE CARD TO CHANGE YOUR LIFE

The Devil resides in each and every one of us. Manifest his energy to confront your own evil nature and capabilities, and so understand yourself better. Banish the Devil to vanquish that evil nature.

This five-card Devil spread will help you understand your dark side, the little devil that we heed when we ignore the angel of conscience. Expand to a 15-card spread by drawing five cards for Body, Mind and Spirit.

- **CARD 1** Who am I?
- **CARD 2** What is the Devil in me?
- **CARD 3** Who or what torments me?
- **CARD 4** Why?
- **CARD 5** What is the resolution?

EXAMPLE READING

CARD 1 2 OF SWORDS: This card points to stalemate. At this time I feel unable to make decisions – I face a choice, but neither option is acceptable to me. However, it may be better to make some kind of decision rather than none at all, which is also a choice of sorts. | **CARD 2** 2 OF COINS: Juggling is the Devil in me. This draw tells me that I enjoy the struggle of balancing several things in the air at once; it makes for excitement. | **CARD 3** 8 OF COINS: This card indicates mastery. I'm tormented by my need to be in control of everything in my life. Sometimes I'm frustrated even when I'm in control because when I'm in control I'm no longer juggling and it's not interesting any more. | **CARD 4** 3 OF SWORDS: Heartache and even heartbreak are symbolized here. I have some unfinished business from a past, painful relationship that I need to deal with before I can move forward with my life. | **CARD 5** 7 OF SWORDS: Drawing this card as my solution suggests that I have been deceiving myself in some way. I need to take a good hard look at myself and my situation. It's time to start being true to myself.

The Tower

16

The destruction of the journey

Lightning strikes the Fool. Perhaps he was standing out in the open, heedless of the warning signs in the weather. The Tower crumbles; bricks and bodies rain down. Now is the time to demolish whatever you ended with the Death card. Destroy the false images and expectations others have of you, pick yourself up and seek a completely new and unexpected direction. By embracing the upheaval, you can move forward on your journey with renewed hope. The alternative is to be dragged through the mud as a passive victim, wondering where you are and how you got there.

Have you ever longed to tear something down and start over from the beginning? The Tower allows you to do just that. Like a hurricane that whips up out of nowhere and leaves devastation in its wake, this archetype returns everything to nothing. You may have lost your job, a relationship, or your peace of mind. However difficult the experience, loss of any kind has the power to open your way to a new positive circumstance. Once beyond the Tower, you may discover you have moved in a direction that you would previously never have dared consider.

REVERSED MEANING

The change I have to face has been delayed, although it's definitely on its way | This isn't a good point to instigate major change | I'm stuck in a rut and going through the same negative experience yet again | I should pay more attention to the mental and spiritual aspects of my life.

APPEARANCE
IN A SPREAD

The beautiful thing about the Tower card is that its apparently destructive energy destroys old stagnant habits of thinking and being, and allows you the freedom to pursue your heart's desires and turn them into physical reality. Its appearance urges you to take encouragement from a shocking upheaval in your life, and to look ahead to the new possibilities. Dare to imagine.

USING THE CARD TO CHANGE YOUR LIFE

This is your big change card. Call upon the powerful energies of the Tower to bring on major upheaval for positive effect. Banish the Tower in order to ward off or slow down the process of a huge change in your life that you don't feel ready to embrace.

Use this exercise when you cannot derive any clear conclusions from performing a large multi-card reading, or after carrying out several smaller readings on the same subject. This is the one to opt for when you are really struggling with an issue and just cannot 'get it'. If you haven't performed any readings but want to carry out the exercise anyway, build your tower by pulling cards from the top of the deck until the Tower falls.

- Take the cards from the reading(s) and start to build yourself a card tower. A flat, non-slippery surface will help you balance the cards.

- As you build your tower, open yourself to change and upheaval. Ask the universe to show you what change it is you need to embrace.

- When the tower of cards falls, as it certainly will, observe the card that lands topmost or any card that flies out.

- This card symbolizes the change you need to work with, whatever your intuition tells you it is. Use this card to meditate on and accept what lies ahead.

- Build up the tower again to see if you get a different result.

17 The Star

The inspiration of the journey

The naked woman that is used in many tarot decks to denote the Star symbolizes the mind, the unconscious, the soul, and all esoteric and intangible energies and realities. The water flowing from the urns she holds represents the ebb and flow of life and health and also movement and change. Perched behind her in the tree, the owl can be read as a reminder of the divine who loves and helps us. The stars themselves, shining so brightly from above, depict the infinite universe and the ideal of heaven. In combination, these symbols communicate divine inspiration in any of its forms, be that creative muse or religious experience.

This card exhorts you to listen to the inspiration that comes from within. You are the Goddess. You have everything you need to achieve your desires. Go for it; don't wait a minute longer. But the Star also holds a warning: consider carefully where you place your energies and time. What's the use of pouring water on water? If you were to pour that same water onto land, you could create a garden that would bear fruit.

REVERSED MEANING

I'm not listening to the Goddess within | Inspiration is stifled or blocked | This isn't a useful time to act on inspiration | I am taking inspiration from my muse for my work or craft, without giving anything back. Prayer, meditation, praise, thanks and appreciation are all ways to nourish the muse. I need to acknowledge that inspiration comes from something greater than myself and be grateful.

APPEARANCE
IN A SPREAD

The Star serves as a reminder that you are the physical embodiment of your spiritual life. Make of your life a work of art. Surround yourself with art and beauty, and realize that this is important. Give gifts that bring aesthetic pleasure.

USING THE STAR TO CHANGE YOUR LIFE

Manifest the Star to call your muse. Banish the Star to remove the hassles of stardom; always being open to the inspirational guidance of your muse, always being passionate, always being true to yourself, can be exhausting.

Try the following when you want to establish a new or deeper connection with your muse or inner Goddess. Have a pen and paper handy.

- Find the Star card in your deck and place it in the centre of your workspace.
- Decide how many points you want to work with on your Star. Five and eight are both good numbers. Shuffle the deck and place that many cards around the Star card.
- Gaze at the layout before you and let your eyes blur and your attention lose focus.
- Open yourself to your inner voice that is your inner Star, your muse.
- Refocus on the layout and take note of patterns and similarities in the colours, shapes and symbols. Notice the relationships between the cards. Is there a progression of numbers that inspires you? A sense of up and down or a flow of energy that runs through the layout?
- Write down your thoughts. This is what the Star has to say to you today.

The Moon

18

The illusion of the journey

The Moon illuminates the night and casts murky shadows. Who can say whether that shape you see from your window is a person stealing toward your house or a tree swaying in a breeze? The Moon wields an unearthly power. It pulls at the water in our bodies as surely as the ocean tides. It draws out our 'shadow self', the evil side of each of us that is usually hidden away and controlled.

This other facet of your character is a necessary part of you. You can accept it and even embrace it using the Moon card as your tool. Don't be ashamed of your darker nature because it has many useful qualities. It steps in when the sunny side of your personality is inadequate for the task at hand. It protects you when no one else will. It gets the difficult jobs done.

Alternatively, interpret the Moon's symbolism as positive and illuminating. Schedule manifestation work and holidays to coincide with its phases rather than the Sun's. Associate it with the calm serenity of the night and the peacefulness of walking your own path.

REVERSED MEANING

I don't have a clue. Life is a lot more complicated than it appears | I'm wasting time shadow-boxing | This is not a fortuitous time for what I have planned. It's the wrong phase of the moon | I'm shying away from my shadow self. Some kind of confrontation is going to be required.

APPEARANCE
IN A SPREAD

The Moon tells you to watch out for what may be lurking in the shadows. Things aren't always what they seem. You may think you know everything about something or someone, but knowledge is always incomplete and therefore uncertain.

USING THE MOON TO CHANGE YOUR LIFE

Manifest the energies of the Moon to commence work with your shadow self (see below). Banish the energies of the Moon to rid yourself of unhelpful illusions.

The following five-card Moon phase not only gives you four new viewpoints from which to consider your question, but also makes you more aware of the phases of our celestial neighbour.

- Choose a card that describes the problem or issue you are working with. Place it in the centre of your workspace.
- Deal four more cards around that central card, as illustrated. Work through the cards and their meanings one at a time.
- **CARD 1** The issue in question.
- **CARD 2** Full Moon. What is obvious about the issue.
- **CARD 3** Waning Moon. What is leaving.
- **CARD 4** New Moon. What is hidden about the issue.
- **CARD 5** Waxing Moon. What is coming next.

19

The Sun

The light of the journey

In sunlight, the shadows are sharp and clear. It's far easier to distinguish right from wrong. The Sun reveals all and forces you to face the truth of your thoughts and actions. You can't hide anything in its bright light. An innocent child has no need to fear exposure. The bearer of a guilty conscience, on the other hand, flinches under the Sun's rays, experiencing them as harsh and glaring.

Before the advent of electricity made the night as bright as day, the rhythms of society and culture were defined by the sun. The day began and ended at her dictate. Sunrise signals work and activity. Sunlight nourishes flowers and crops. It stirs up the winds that bring fresh air. It feels good on your skin and warms the muscles beneath. Every day, sunrise gives us the hope of a second chance and a fresh start. Today you can make things better. High noon is the time of activity and appetite: today you can get things done. Sunset brings a slow down, a pause before we welcome the night. Tonight you can relax because you did well.

REVERSED MEANING

Someone means to rain on my parade | I'm not feeling as carefree as I would like. There's discord where there should be harmony | I've worked myself so hard, I'm in danger of burnout. I need to cool things down | Aspects of my situation are the reverse of safe and nurturing.

APPEARANCE IN A SPREAD

This card appears to tell you to see your situation anew with a child's simple, unprejudiced vision. Remember how magical your childhood was, when each day was crammed with new life experiences and each moment was precious. Use that sunny, intense view of the world to bring a fresh perspective.

USING THE SUN TO CHANGE YOUR LIFE

Harness the Sun's brilliance to manifest clarity of sight and second sight. Banish the Sun to dispel painfully harsh visions and to dull distressing memories.

Use this four-card sunlight spread to explore how you are perceived by other people, or lay it out in relation to a specific person or circumstance.

- Shuffle your deck, deal four cards and arrange them in a line to resemble a ray of sunshine.
- **CARD 1** The Sun. The face you put on for others.
- **CARD 2** The Light. What others perceive about you.
- **CARD 3** The Corona. The direct effect you have on others.
- **CARD 4** The Solar Wind. The subtle effect you have on others.

EXAMPLE READING

CARD 1 2 OF WANDS: This card signifies dominion. I like others to perceive me as someone who owns and controls a lot of things, as someone who takes on many projects. I am efficient, I've got it together and I take responsibility seriously. | **CARD 2** KING OF CUPS: My second card represents mature emotion. Other people see me as calm, cool and collected in the midst of fire; as loving and affectionate by nature; as able to express my feelings honestly. People know what they are getting with me. There's no hidden agenda. | **CARD 3** 5 OF COINS (REVERSED): This card tells me that I help people see adversity as a challenge. I turn setbacks into opportunities and encourage others to do the same. | **CARD 4** 11 STRENGTH (REVERSED): My final card tells me that the subtle effect I have on others is one of tough love (weak control). People are forced to a higher standard of behaviour by my no-nonsense practicality.

Judgement

The realization of the journey

In the Vedic tradition of ancient India, one of two types of beings comes for the soul at the end of life, either Vishnudutas or Yamadutas. Their function is to escort the soul to its next stage of existence. In Christianity, an archangel blows his horn to summon the soul to rise from the grave. Both examples function as a metaphor for awakening to the higher purpose in your life. Take a look at the long expanse of your life and judge what you have done, what you have accomplished, and what yet needs to be done. Rise again and reinvent yourself.

Exercising judgement means being able to discriminate and make intelligent choices. In an ideal world, humans make choices and use their judgement in the service of a higher, noble purpose. Perhaps the most noble purpose is to help others.

Mother Teresa said: 'If you judge people, you have no time to love them.' Her life displayed a higher purpose. The Judgement card of the tarot is about acknowledging your higher power and your higher purpose; remembering it and living your life in accordance with it. Be merciful to yourself and others.

REVERSED MEANING

Somehow the communication channel that links me to my higher power is blocked | I have been distracted and so strayed from the true purpose of my life | It is not appropriate to show mercy in this instance | Am I ignoring my higher calling when I should be doing something far more important?

APPEARANCE
IN A SPREAD

When the Judgement card makes an appearance, it reminds you to heed the call of your own higher power. In some way or another, you are being called to judge a person or situation. Show mercy because you may be judged by the same standard.

USING JUDGEMENT TO CHANGE YOUR LIFE

Call upon the energy of the Judgement card to discover your spiritual calling. Banish its energy to be rid of the old life and a way of doing things that is no longer effective.

You can pass judgement on yourself over and over again for the same crime committed a long time ago. If you're not careful, condemning yourself to failure becomes an ingrained habit. Put a stop to a negative cycle by using this seven-card judgement spread. Once you learn to be merciful with yourself, you'll be better able to show mercy to others. Pick your seven cards at random.

- **CARD 1** Why do I judge myself so harshly?
- **CARD 2** To whom does this condemning voice in my head actually belong?
- **CARD 3** Is there another condemning voice?
- **CARD 4** What is the truth of the matter?
- **CARD 5** Why do I deserve mercy?
- **CARD 6** How can I end this non-progressive cycle?
- **CARD 7** How can I move forward from here?

The World

The integration of the journey

At last the Fool has come full circle in his journey, having learned his lessons well. He is complete, existing in harmony with the universe. Everything has come together and the outlook couldn't be more positive. The World is the integrated whole, an assimilation of the truths and experiences of all the major arcana. Your life is in a stable state of balance and completeness. You have passed the test. Make a record of your journey to share with others on the path. Take some time to acknowledge your achievements and give yourself a reward. Consider how you can pass on your hard-earned wisdom.

The World card of the tarot, along with the Sun, the Moon and the Star, suggests astronomy and astrology and the natural rhythms of the cosmos. The sun and the moon undoubtedly influence our mood and energy. Many people are familiar with the effect of Mercury retrograde – Mercury appearing to move backward through the zodiac – on communications and mechanical devices. The World links us to all the planets in our solar system, and encourages us to seek out the effects those planets have on us and our world.

REVERSED MEANING

I'm still looking for integration and wholeness in my life | I haven't reached the end of this particular cycle. The finish line may not even be in sight | Although I consider myself wise in theory, I haven't managed to assimilate that wisdom in my daily life | My horoscope points to a time of struggle.

APPEARANCE IN A SPREAD

The World indicates a sense of completeness and stability in a situation or person. The end stage has been reached. Now is the time to put knowledge into practice, spread your wisdom, or just enjoy the sensation

USING THE WORLD TO CHANGE YOUR LIFE

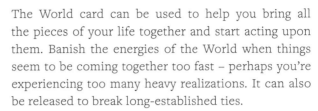

The World card can be used to help you bring all the pieces of your life together and start acting upon them. Banish the energies of the World when things seem to be coming together too fast – perhaps you're experiencing too many heavy realizations. It can also be released to break long-established ties.

This exercise will reveal your four tasks for wholeness. Shuffle, cut and deal the cards to discover the four things you need in order to claim the World.

- **CARD 1** Search this out. This is something you need. It involves going somewhere or doing something new. It may be meeting a new person.
- **CARD 2** Accept this gift. It's something that you have denied yourself for far too long. Enjoy it.
- **CARD 3** Give this gift. In giving, we receive. So many things can be given away that are never lost – love, jokes, mercy, kindness, a smile.
- **CARD 4** Seek this within. It's something you already have, but have yet to acknowledge. It's an aspect of your inner wisdom that has seen you through many times, a strength that you didn't realize you possessed.

EXAMPLE READING

In this example, the four cards are all courts, and three are reversed. The courts may refer to four different people in the querent's life or four facets of the querent's personality. When the majority of cards in a reading are reversed, there is an overall block in the energy of the situation, which means a major effort has to be made to achieve the desired result.

CARD 1 KING OF COINS (REVERSED): I need to seek out and accept help from someone who is adept, but doesn't show it externally (because the card is reversed). Or perhaps I need to seek out a new income stream, as suggested by the Coins suit. | **CARD 2** KNIGHT OF CUPS (REVERSED): Reversed, my gift is probably the absence of something. It may be that I have not been invited to a gathering. I should accept this and fill that time with an activity I enjoy. | **CARD 3** KNIGHT OF WANDS (REVERSED): The Knight in reverse tells me to help someone who is burned out, or exhausted. I can give a gift of understanding. | **CARD 4** QUEEN OF WANDS: I should trust in the qualities of the Queen that I see in myself. The fire inside me shines on, energizing all who know me.

chapter two
The Minor Arcana

The minor arcana of the tarot are divided into four suits: Wands, Cups, Swords and Coins. Depending on your choice of deck, Wands are sometimes known as Staffs, Staves, Batons or Clubs; Cups are sometimes called Chalices, Vessels, Goblets or Hearts; Swords are also known as Knives, Arrows, Blades and Spades; and Coins are sometimes called Circles, Pentacles or Diamonds.

Each of the four suits contains ten numbered cards, also called pips, and four court cards. The symbolic meaning of each depends on its suit derivation and its number. There are various systems of symbolism. For simplicity, we will use a system in which Wands represent elemental Fire because wood fuels fire; Cups symbolize Water because vessels hold liquids; Swords symbolize Air because swords, knives and arrowheads are swung or fly through the air towards their target; Coins symbolize the Earth because they are made from metal, which is derived from ore or earth. This Elemental system provides a rich vocabulary that will allow us to imbue picture, colour and detail with deep personal meaning.

Wands Fire | Passion

If you were to lay out all the cards in the Wands suit from 1, or the Ace, to 10, you would have everything required to describe and explore the areas in your life that are touched by passion, intuition, willpower, action, the yang principle, love and strength, truth and justice – any aspect that relates to Fire. You might choose to relate your job or career to these cards, along with your relationships, the summer season, the time of high noon, the direction south, and anything pertaining to gut instinct.

Cups Water | Emotion

The Cups cards show up in readings where the issues at stake pertain mainly to emotions, feelings and relationships. The energies contained in this suit relate to Water. Water flows, is dynamic and changeable; it cleanses and heals. The season associated with Cups is autumn, sunset is its time, and west is the direction. Laid out from 1 to 10, this suit could tell the story of a relationship: from its beginning to its fulfilment.

Swords Air | Intellect

The Swords suit relates to the brain and intellect, the simple act of breathing, and the senses that depend on Air, namely sight, smell and sound. Most tarot decks show the Swords as double-edged, meaning they can cut away the good as well as the bad. The appearance of a Sword tends to indicate some kind of dilemma that has no easy black-and-white resolution and so requires a tough decision. Swords is the suit of spring, the time is sunrise, and the direction is east.

Coins Earth | Physicality

Cards belonging to the Coins suit relate to the home, health, money, basic survival, prosperity, accomplishments and the energies of greed, poverty and ill health. The element represented here is Earth, associated with all that is solid, stable and reliable. The 'story' related by the Coins cards could be a new job or a physical endeavour. The season is winter, the time is midnight, and the direction is north.

THE COURT CARDS

The court cards function as a bridge between the common experience of the pips and the extraordinary life-changing experiences of the majors. All the energies of the suit are assimilated as the progression is made from Page to King. The Page is immature, the Knight is active, the Queen is emotionally mature and nurturing, and the King is wisely mature and accomplished. In the pagan wheel of the year, the last day of October symbolizes Death. Six weeks of quiet time follow until the winter solstice, when a spark of new life takes hold. The court cards fall into that period between ending and beginning: a time to mull over things; to experience ending in full, and perhaps also loss; to embrace the lessons learned until newfound wisdom is manifest in your everyday actions and thoughts, to the extent that you aren't conscious of it any more.

Ace ☩ Birth

Aces relate to the Fool and, to some extent, the Pages, being concerned with new beginnings and immaturity. The Ace can be viewed as a one-dimensional representation of the story of each suit. It holds all the qualities and energies of its designation in potential. The Ace steps forward and says, 'Once upon a time...'. It's your choice whether to let its energy move you forward or backward on your path, or not to move at all. There's simply no way of knowing how it will turn out in the end.

THE ACE OF WANDS

This Ace symbolizes the emergence of action, passion and will, whether in a sexual relationship, a new project, or other area of your life.

Wands are fiery and masculine. The Ace can indicate that you are about to take on a role as a father figure or role model, or else that you need to embrace and utilize your strength and assertiveness.

REVERSED MEANING

A reversed card indicates that the potential for power is present, but is not being realized. The force is being blocked by a situation, an action or a non-action. It may be that you are not taking responsibility for your own power. If the question asked concerns another person, this may indicate that they are not an appropriate sexual partner, or role model.

THE ACE OF CUPS

The appearance of this Ace represents the first stirrings of a new emotion or relationship. The relationship may be friendly, romantic or just a casual acquaintance made at the supermarket. This new emotion you feel may not even involve another person, but instead be a change in yourself. Your happiness is the first consideration. Let the Ace encourage you to do what makes you feel good.

REVERSED MEANING

A reversed card suggests you are failing to recognize a budding emotion or relationship, and so may miss a valuable opportunity. Or perhaps now is not an appropriate time to follow the deepest desires of your heart. In this case, you are best advised to hold out until circumstances are more favourable.

THE ACE OF SWORDS

This Ace signals the start of some kind of mental process or moral dilemma. When I see it in a reading, I suggest the querent consider their ethics, morals and standards.

An alternative way to read the Ace is as permission to develop a new thought or idea, to take a walk down some untried mental avenue. Take it as confirmation that a new idea you have had is a good one.

REVERSED MEANING

A reversed card could indicate that your new idea is not a sensible one, or perhaps that initiative is being blocked in some way. If this reading isn't appropriate, the message may be that you are entering murky ethical or moral waters. Your sense of right and wrong is being challenged and compromised. It may be time to make some tough decisions.

THE ACE OF COINS

This lucky card points to prosperity and as such is a great one to get in a reading if you are considering a new business endeavour. It's an auspicious sign in general, symbolizing new opportunity and a favourable prospect for any existing physical or monetary plan. Accept this Ace gladly as good news for your health, wealth and home.

REVERSED MEANING

The advice of this Ace in reverse is that now is a good time to save money rather than spend it. It suggests a need for preventative medicine, like a 'flu vaccination or vitamin and mineral supplements, and for you to get back into shape.

2 ‡ Pair

The energy of the number 2 is balance. It is a pair, a duet, a deuce, double trouble, twins. Its nature is dual and linear, as in up/down, in/out, coming/going. The card adjacent to the number 2 in a reading confirms which of the two paths has been taken. You may decide it's time to change direction.

2 OF WANDS

The 2 of Wands suggests the possibilities your intuition can bring, the responsibilities that are inseparable from true authority, or the power struggle of a relationship. Will you be the one to lead or follow?

This 2 is strongly masculine and asks you to examine your responsibilities and to evaluate the care you give to all and everything in your dominion.

REVERSED MEANING

Reversed, this 2 tells you that your responsibilities are too much, or that they exceed the extent of your authority. We all know what it's like to shoulder all the responsibility and have none of the authority.

Or perhaps there is a problem with something you have responsibility for. What have you neglected lately? Alternatively, the problem revealed may lie in a relationship in which the balance of power is inappropriate.

2 OF CUPS

The 2 of Cups is the archetype of a balanced, harmonious relationship and so is an excellent indicator of romance and marriage. In other contexts, the 2 can herald a favourable working relationship, friendship, and so on. It symbolizes all those things that make a relationship work: clear communication, cooperation, loyalty, sharing, consideration and, of course, true love and affection.

REVERSED MEANING

Reversed, the 2 tells you that this may not be the ideal partnership after all. The natural flow of cooperation is not present. Loyalty, affection and true love are not manifest – although they may develop, given effort.

The perfect pair is off-balance in a reversed reading. Could the reason be a third party in this relationship?

2 OF SWORDS

Generally speaking, the Swords are quick and decisive, dealing out decisions or pain as swift as thought, but the 2 is a card of stalemate, stagnation and indecision. It is as though it is being pulled in both directions at once. In a reading, this card often indicates there are no good choices to be made, but it may also mean that there are no bad decisions.

The energy leads into the 3 by offering the choice to make no choice at all.

REVERSED MEANING

Reversed, the 2 confirms you have made a decision, or that a decision has been made for you and is out of your hands. Perhaps you have accepted the intellectual gift of the Ace, but are not moving forward with it in a positive direction. You may need to engage more fully in the creative process.

2 OF COINS

The 2 in the Coins suit is often concerned with juggling money or time. The balance maintained in this case is apt to tumble at any moment, taking you back to 1 or on to 3. Extended, the juggling theme can apply to any area of your life, whether that means finding the right balance between your material and spiritual life, or giving enough to both work and family.

REVERSED MEANING

Reversed, the 2 warns that your balancing act is in jeopardy. You can no longer rob Peter to pay Paul. You are going to be pulled in one direction for a time before you can find balance again.

3 ‡ Growth

Add an upward line (or z axis) to the two-dimensional plane created by the Ace and the 2 and you enter the third dimension. The energy of the 3s grows out of the balanced state of the 2s in a variety of interesting ways. It's a thrice, a trio, a trey, triplet, triplex, and comes in triplicate. A 3 signifies expansion, reaching outward from the sturdy base provided by the 2. Have you noticed that it isn't just bad things that come in threes?

3 OF WANDS

The weight of dominion in the 2 now ventures outward in exploration. Whether it's a relationship, a job or career, or your personal power that is in question, the 3 of Wands means you need to keep on with the quest. There's more treasure out there to be found, and it's too early to be making decisions and commitments. Explore the great unknown; reach beyond your present boundaries. Look for clues as though on a scavenger hunt. Your higher power will illuminate the signposts.

REVERSED MEANING

Reversed, this card tells you that exploratory energy is blocked somehow and for some purpose. Perhaps it's not an advisable time for far-flung exploration, or maybe your own timidity is preventing it. This 3 indicates a barrier to new possibilities.

3 OF CUPS

The 3 of Cups makes easy transition from the stable partnership of the 2 with the addition of a child or friend. This card tells of family, society, community and the joy we find in sharing our self with others. Other people provide a useful mirror in which to see yourself more clearly. The message is get out, meet new people and party!

REVERSED MEANING

Reversed, the 3 of Cups warns you to be circumspect in the company you keep. It's sometimes appropriate to be sceptical and a little suspicious of a new person. Trust your feelings and pull back from socializing or joining new groups when this 3 appears.

3 OF SWORDS

The 3 of Swords is the heartbreak card. The 2 tells us that there is no good decision to be made, so disappointment and sadness are a natural next step. It's hard for people to allow themselves to feel pain. We want to go on as though it doesn't bother us, as though nothing serious has taken place. But pain is real and has to be faced straight on, accepted and assimilated before it can truly be laid down and forgotten. This card may mean pain is on its way or is present and must be accepted.

REVERSED MEANING

Reversed, the heartache of the card is mitigated or lessened. This isn't the great drama you thought it was going to be. The 3 can also indicate self-pity, moroseness or some other negative emotion. Another way to interpret it is as an admonishment not to give in to heartache, or let sorrow sway your decisions.

3 OF COINS

The 3 of Coins describes cooperation between three parties, or some kind of group effort, like the fund raising, planning and physical execution of any major project or job. This card is apprenticeship, the 8 of Coins represents mastery, and the King of Coins is an adept. As such, the 3 has connotations of the journeyman. Its appearance can point to skilled workmanship, and indicate a reward for hard work, such as a pay increase or a better job.

REVERSED MEANING

Reversed, the 3 of Coins warns you that the pay rise you were counting on might not come through after all. There is a downturn in the progress of a project, downsizing planned in the company, or slump in the economy.

4 ✦ Balance

Let's go beyond the three tangible physical dimensions and add time to define a fourth dimension. We can learn from the past, look forward and plan for the future, or be fully present in the now. The four-sided square is an especially stable, balanced shape; there are four seasons in the year, four cardinal directions, four main times of day, and four suits in the tarot. Four is a quartet, a quadratic equation, quadruple the fun, a foursome and a fourfold path to freedom.

4 OF WANDS

The 4 of Wands is a celebration of freedom. Take time to enjoy the fruits of the exploration you performed in service of the 3. Add that four-poled gazebo or pavilion to the garden; it'll be fun. This celebration is well deserved; your freedom has been won through struggle. The plateau you have reached has been attained through personal power.

REVERSED MEANING

Reversed, the 4 of Wands suggests it's not yet time to party. There is one last thing blocking your freedom. Maybe the people you want to celebrate with aren't feeling the same as you do. Take their feelings and situation into consideration.

4 OF CUPS

The 4 of Cups points to excess. It conveys a sense of emotional burnout, perhaps the result of too much socializing at the behest of the 3. Meeting new people and spending time with them can be draining. The 3 of Cups can be so full, you can't even bring yourself to look at the fourth, and therefore could miss out on an opportunity or a gift. Give yourself some time to clear out the excess.

REVERSED MEANING

Reversed, the 4 of Cups tells you that excess isn't your problem, or else that the feeling you are experiencing is dissipating rapidly. Cups placed upside down let their contents run out and flow away. Time could well be running out.

4 OF SWORDS

The 4 of Swords urges you to rest, recuperate, recharge, recycle, regrow and recover. Take note, all of these require action; you won't achieve them just by sitting still long enough. One of the reasons there is so much tension, stress and anxiety in the modern, technological world is because people do not know how to rest and recharge themselves. For some, recovery means an energetic game of squash, for others it's incense and candles at 4 a.m. Discover what works best for you.

REVERSED MEANING

Reversed, this card indicates that something or someone is preventing your much-needed rest. You could be suffering from insomnia or maybe you can never sit still because your mind is always racing.

Time makes you even more anxious: there isn't enough of it to indulge all your fantastic ideas.

4 OF COINS

The 4 of Coins puts the spotlight on possessiveness and reveals the way you relate to your possessions. Do you take good care of them and are you willing to share them? This card is about acquiring more than you truly need, which is fine in times of plenty. It is also a warning not to treat people as possessions.

REVERSED MEANING

Reversed, the 4 of Coins warns you to keep greedy tendencies in check. You are never satisfied and live your life thinking 'I have so much, yet I only want more'. You believe that your time is more important than anyone else's and you are impatient to achieve your goals.

5 ‡ Challenge

Much as we'd like to remain within the solid square of the 4, the path is to face challenge and struggle. The 5s take you into the intangible dimensions of mind, spirit and ego, the realm of the fifth element or fifth sacred thing. Here is the pentagon, pentacle, pentagram and the quintet, the fivefold path, a fifth wheel and the fifth column. The 5s in the tarot symbolize everything that disturbs the peace contained within the 4s, leading toward the growth, maturity and fruitfulness represented by the higher numbers.

5 OF WANDS

This card brings with it notions of healthy competition, constructive criticism and enjoyable debate. It invites you to test your power, will and skill in competition with others. Cooperation is key when people of different backgrounds and with different ideas come together. Expand yourself to accommodate foreign paradigms.

REVERSED MEANING

Reversed, the 5 of Wands signals bad communication, ill will and a general lack of cooperation. It may be that the contest you are engaged in is rigged and there is no option but defeat. It may also indicate that the criticism you are receiving or dispensing is ill founded. Ask yourself if the fight is worth it in the long run.

5 OF CUPS

The appearance of this 5 asks you to consider your sanity. Are you about to do something you might regret? Consider your options carefully, and know that you explored every angle of your predicament before proceeding.

The 5 of Cups is a warning, so be patient with yourself in your decision making. Give yourself time to act out of wisdom, rather than on impulse or out of desperation.

REVERSED MEANING

Read in reverse, this 5 is a friendly admonishment: 'Stop beating yourself up. There is nothing to regret. You did the best you could with what you had at the time.' Take it as an order to put the past behind you and move on.

5 OF SWORDS

The 5 of the Swords suggests that you have a loss to face. Whatever the battle, the odds are stacked against you. Remember that, for every victory, every winner, there has to be a defeat and a loser, perhaps many losers. Or it may be that the struggle indicated by the card is an intellectual one. Consider getting help to figure out the solution, but choose your helper wisely.

REVERSED MEANING

Hope is not lost if the 5 is reversed. You still have time and opportunity to turn the situation into a victory. Be advised that snatching victory from the jaws of defeat takes enormous energy.

5 OF COINS

This 5 pertains to a genuine, unavoidable lack and can indicate ill health. It's a bad sign in regard to acquiring money or other forms of wealth. Something serious in your life needs to be faced and taken care of, or accepted if that's the only option. The appearance of this 5 can also highlight physical addiction.

REVERSED MEANING

Good news: the loss isn't as bad as you first thought. There might be a way to get round it. The lack symbolized by the upright card hasn't impacted yet. You may still have a chance to prevent it.

6 ⁜ Resolution

Six sides and six angles make up the hexagon. When struggling with the challenges of the 5s, take six deep breaths and look at your problem from at least six different angles. Imagine six different solutions, no matter how preposterous. The 6s of the suits come as a welcome relief after the intensity of the 5s. View them as the resolution of the struggle as you continue up the path of pips. Consider that the sixth chakra is your third eye, the seat of your psychic vision, as well as the mind and all functions of the brain and head. (See pages 148–51 for more about chakras.)

6 OF WANDS

Congratulations! The 6 of Wands announces that victory is yours. You have won that power struggle and can now be open to positive communication. Let your mind as well as your ears be receptive to good news and be ready to act upon it. Be ready to accept praise graciously with a 'Thank you', rather than the usual 'Think nothing of it', for they will.

Appreciate your own worth and value and expect others to do the same.

REVERSED MEANING

Reversed, the 6 of Wands warns that others will criticize or second-guess the way you handled a situation, discounting or belittling your success. This card's appearance is bad news. It reeks of success without satisfaction, and damnation with faint praise.

6 OF CUPS

This 6 evokes the innocence of days gone by. It's all right to indulge in nostalgia and memories. Your current mental state is built upon the emotions you experienced in your childhood. Understanding the past is the answer to a great many questions. Receive gifts and advice in the spirit in which they are given, without adding contextual meaning. Innocently extend the benefit of the doubt.

REVERSED MEANING

Reversed, this 6 advises you to be wary of people and situations which seem innocent. Allow yourself some healthy scepticism. Another interpretation is a warning not to linger or dwell in the past. You can get hung up on history to the detriment of the here and now. Let your heart and mind explore the present.

6 OF SWORDS

The 6 of Swords heralds change and travel. It's up to you whether the change is permanent or temporary. You tried one idea and took it to its logical conclusion – this card tells you it's time for Plan B. A trip or vacation will give you a different perspective. Grab any opportunity for travel and a change of scenery.

REVERSED MEANING

This 6 reversed indicates a wrong turn and a need to backtrack. The travel plans you have are either inappropriate or unproductive. Instead of enjoying a pleasant change of scene, you are leaving calm waters for choppy seas.

6 OF COINS

The 6 of the Earth element is about having enough to give away, being generous and kind, and helping out. Your acceptance of, or victory over, the lack embodied in the 5 has meant you now have more than enough in other areas. Concentrate on your strengths. Utilize what you have. Share and give whenever you can, even if anonymously.

REVERSED MEANING

Reversed, the 6 of Coins tells you to see other people as worthy of your gifts, and not yourself as superior for having something to give. False pride is as insidious and destructive as false humility.

7 ‡ Possibility

Do you have a lucky number? Seven is mine. I get excited whenever I see a seven because, with this number on my side, I know anything is possible. The energy of the 7s concerns expanding your quality of life and making your life a work of art. The 7s take us forward to a higher level. There are seven main chakras (energy centres) in the body, and wholeness is achieved by balancing, energizing and realizing the full potential of all seven. Seventh heaven is the condition of perfect happiness.

7 OF WANDS

The 7 of Wands indicates that defiance is a good thing. Right is on your side, so go ahead and fight the good fight. Stand up for your ideals and what you believe in. Realize that you feel passionate about your principles and refuse to act against them. This card confirms that the time is right to stand firm. You have reached a solid position from which to defeat energies that seek to pull you from your course.

REVERSED MEANING

This 7 in reverse argues that you don't have the higher ground, or you are about to lose it. You might want to reconsider your original plan.

Another interpretation is that you don't have the passion and will to sustain this struggle. Events are leading you astray and it will take tremendous effort to regain your former, righteous position.

7 OF CUPS

The 7 in the realm of air symbolizes imagination. It tells you to go ahead and dare to dream. Why not actually live the dream? Set your imagination to work. Allow yourself to contemplate the wildest ideas and emotions, then act on them to enrich your life as well as your relationships. Let your heart expand. Seek beauty and see the beauty of others.

REVERSED MEANING

The other side of the 7 card can indicate that you are letting your imagination run wild and being totally impractical. The scenarios and attainments you envisage might never be. Reel in your mind and heart.

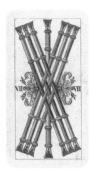

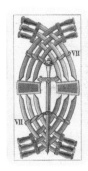

7 OF SWORDS

This 7 alludes to mental confusion. It tells you to watch out for the tendency we all have to cheat or bend the truth. It can also warn of others who may be seeking to take advantage.

The 7 of Swords is probably the biggest 'red flag' in the deck. Generally speaking, it's a giant caution sign. Be careful! Stay safe!

REVERSED MEANING

Reversed, the 7 of Swords assures you that, while everything isn't completely above board, you have nothing to fear. The appearance of this card should allay suspicions about theft and dishonesty. It also indicates the presence of an outcast or someone who doesn't fit in.

7 OF COINS

Take this card as affirmation that you've done everything right in the garden of life. You have tilled the earth, planted good seeds, fertilized and watered on schedule, and rooted out any weeds as you've gone along. Now you simply have to wait for the fruit to ripen. Be patient because there's no hurrying the process. Take pleasure in watching your garden grow.

REVERSED MEANING

Read in reverse, the 7 of Coins means you haven't done everything you should have. You need to start nurturing the garden of your life and pull up the weeds of laziness, procrastination and waste.

8 ✦ Balance

The energy of eight has twice the solidity of a four-sided square, and three orders of magnitude of the balance of a pair. The 8 of tarot is so solid and stable that many mistake it for an end or the completion of a process. The figure of eight on its side is the symbol for infinity, which is the greatest of all things. Look at the 8s as a plateau on the journey rather than an ultimate peak, even if it appears whole and complete. It signifies that you have reached and realized the possibilities extended by the 7s.

8 OF WANDS

The 8 of Wands points to the timely arrival of aid, strength and inspiration in your righteous struggle. Here comes your second wind. Something will happen soon and most likely in your favour. The card reveals that ethereal energies are grounding into practical actions and deeds. Now is an auspicious time to move forward with your plans.

REVERSED MEANING

Reversed, this 8 highlights serious delay. For some reason, help is not arriving and you need to figure out why, or else keep going without it. You cannot count on expectations. The energies are working against you, so keep a low profile for a while.

8 OF CUPS

The 8 of the Cups suit suggests it's time to let go of the things and emotions that you are finished with. Honour them, but leave them behind and move upward and onward to better things. This card regularly makes an appearance when the querent is considering ending a relationship. I read it as a sign that there is really no sense in trying to hold on to something that is no longer there.

REVERSED MEANING

Reversed, this 8 says that you are not yet ready to move on. You are still mulling over many emotions and aspects of the relationship. The energy of the card is sinking backward and downward. The likelihood is that you can't see how to end the relationship on a pleasant note.

8 OF SWORDS

The energy of this card is restrictive. Perhaps you are caught in the web of lies spun by the 7. Your choices and actions have now imprisoned you. Only you can get yourself out of this mess. Use your intellect to make good your previous decisions.

There's nothing wrong with changing your mind and words can be retracted. First, admit that you got it wrong.

REVERSED MEANING

Reversed, the 8 of Swords proves that there is a way to exit the prison in which you've found yourself.

Go ahead and try the locks. They may not be as unbreakable as they seem.

8 OF COINS

The 8 of Coins denotes mastery of your craft, career or finances. All that experience and hard work are at last paying off. You are in excellent health and at the top of your game. You are no longer an apprentice or journeyman, your skills are of considerable value. You are the master of your destiny. Draw this card and you know it's a good time to ask for a salary increase or promotion.

REVERSED MEANING

The reverse of this card indicates that someone is posing as a master when they don't have the experience and skills. You may be fooling yourself and overestimating your worth. What have you done lately? Fight complacency.

9 ⊹ Accomplishment

Three threes combine in the 9, and so these cards contain the growth energy of the 3s, the resolution of the 6s, and also the rewards of the 9s. This is your last chance to deal with unfinished business before completion of the cycle. Read a 9 as a sign that it's time to look to the past and reflect on your current place on life's path. Consider that, although the 10 completes the suit, the achievements of the 9 are whole in themselves: if 10 is graduation, 9 is completion of the course.

9 OF WANDS

The 9 of Wands represents the manifestation of will and personal power. You are on the winning side or have already won. Merely persevere and you will gain your desires. The reward for a job well done is another job. Stay on course because the end is in sight. Let the marks left by your struggles be badges of honour and accomplishment.

REVERSED MEANING

Unfortunately, this card indicates that perseverance will most likely not pay dividends. You are fighting a lost cause. The situation is merely draining you of energy and will. The point of diminishing returns has been reached. It's time to bail out and cut your losses.

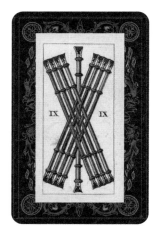

9 OF CUPS

The 9 of the Cups suit is the emotional reward that you get when you are satisfied with yourself. The circumstance you have helped create is good and fulfilling. Relationships are ripe and fruitful. This is the traditional 'wish' card in a reading: indication that your wish will be satisfied and that the wish is appropriate.

REVERSED MEANING

Reversed, the 9 describes a sense of dissatisfaction. It's the sensation you experience when you acquire something you thought you wanted desperately, only to realize it's not what you thought it was. The classic example is a miserable rich person. It also shows itself in high divorce rates. People look to money and a mate for happiness, but true contentment comes from within yourself.

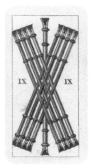

9 OF SWORDS

You have some intellectual work to do before finishing the current cycle, and it's going to be difficult and draining. Worry results in anxiety, self-doubt and sleeplessness. Perhaps you know what the correct decision is for you, but are finding it too painful to act on. If you continue to hesitate, the decision may be taken from you.

REVERSED MEANING

Reversed, the 9 of Swords states that there is no real cause for anxiety and self-doubt. It tells you to re-examine the thoughts that have led you to this state. You'll probably find they have no basis in reality.

The cause of your worry and insomnia may be physical, such as allergies or a change in weather, rather than intellectual.

9 OF COINS

This 9 represents the rewards of prudent choices and work. Its appearance exhorts you to enjoy the results of a life well lived. It may also be taken as an instruction to make sound choices, such as saving regularly and living modestly, so that you can live free from financial worries and enjoy your retirement, unless you are prepared for adversity.

REVERSED MEANING

Read in reverse, the 9 of Coins indicates imprudence or foolish choices that may well lead to financial disaster or illness. It is imperative that you wisen up and take control of your finances and health.

10 ‡ Completion

Ten fingers and ten toes: it's no wonder our numerical system is base ten. Ten is perfection and entirety. Ten tens is one hundred, a century, and ten of those is a millennium. We count ages of history in these terms and the history of our life in decades. The 10 in the tarot means completion. It represents the culmination of the journey in the energies symbolized by its suit. The 10 encompasses all the experiences and challenges that have marked the pips' progress from the Ace onward. The 10 embodies the fulfilment of that suit's purpose.

10 OF WANDS

This 10 represents the strength and will you have to carry a heavy burden, whether this is the joyful responsibility of raising children, the slack of co-workers, or the demands of your own business. This card symbolizes the ultimate test of your willpower and passion. It is the fulfilment of the assertiveness begun with the Ace.

REVERSED MEANING

Reversed, this card suggests that the burden you bear is inappropriate, or that it has become too heavy and unmanageable to be viable. Lighten your load.

10 OF CUPS

The 10 of Cups indicates complete fulfilment of the heart's desires. It denotes true happiness and success in any endeavour. This card may appear in conjunction with the culmination of a relationship or a healing process. It augurs well for the creation of a family, a group or a team, or some other complete unit that will satisfy your heart.

REVERSED MEANING

This 10 in reverse tells you that the likelihood of success is diminished. The matter in question requires more effort and energy. You might have to 'settle', meaning accept things as they are because it's the best the situation has to offer.

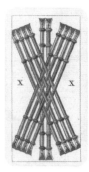

10 OF SWORDS

The 10 of Swords warns that you are about to be confronted with one of the hardest decisions you will ever have to make. Prepare to face the most trying circumstance. Beware of backstabbing and betrayal. Now is the time to admit defeat and beg as you claw your way back up from the depths of depression.

REVERSED MEANING

Reversed, this 10 may mean that rock bottom wasn't quite reached on this occasion. Alternatively, it may signify that what you thought was a betrayal is not, and that the problem is actually one of miscommunication or misunderstanding.

10 OF COINS

The sum of all the Coins represents permanence in home, health, finances and family. When you get this card, you can be assured they are here to stay. Knowledge, love and skills are passed on from one generation to the next. Money, property or land are inherited. Listen to and learn from the experience and wisdom of your elders. Take your appropriate place in the family pageant.

REVERSED MEANING

The flip side of this Coin warns of impermanence. That special something you are counting on just might disappear. Watch your stocks and shares. Make doubly sure that you can afford a big purchase like a house or car before signing the contract.

Page

also known as Princess, Sister or Daughter

In traditional decks, the Page card is illustrated by a young man, who holds the symbol of his suit in his hands. The card's appearance in a reading was sometimes taken to refer to someone in the querent's life who carried messages and ran errands pertaining to the symbolism of that suit. Its appearance was also thought to indicate a young person with the same hair colour as pictured in the card. These days most tarot readers find it more useful to talk in terms of a person's qualities and personality, and to find links between these and the card's symbolism. In many modern decks the Page has been replaced by a Princess, Sister or Daughter who, as well as being distinctly female, doesn't signify a particular age group. A sister may be 8 or 80.

There are many systems of association in use for the courts (and all tarot cards). They can be interpreted as people in the querent's life, or aspects of the querent's character. They can show stations in life, or steps along life's path. As you work with the court cards, you will establish and develop a system that works for you. My court chronology begins in the east (sunrise, spring, air) with a flighty, air-headed Page who has only just begun to assimilate the experience of the previous ten cards of his suit. He has all the promise of a bright sunrise on a spring day at the beach, yet his immaturity means he jumps to conclusions, and often changes his mind according to whim or fancy. The latter isn't such a bad thing; circumstances change and, when they do, flexibility can be useful.

PAGE OF WANDS

Air of Fire | intellectualized will | faith

Affirmation: Faith in myself strengthens my faith in others.

Like a new spouse or parent, the naive Page of Wands really has no idea of the magnitude of the task he has taken on. He steps up eagerly to the task of embracing the ten energies contained from Ace to 10, with all enthusiasm. He's clever and eager to prove himself. He's got it all figured out. He will be tested in every way.

APPEARANCE IN A SPREAD

Belief is strengthened by passing through the Fire of doubt, fear and embarrassing mistakes. One interpretation of the Page of Wands card is that, like a young religious zealot or a new convert, you face a test of faith. The card reminds you to have belief in yourself, others and the divine.

REVERSED MEANING

Reversed, the Page of Wands indicates that faith is truly shaken or isn't based on a firm foundation of trust and experience. Imagine a high wind (Air: Page) whipping at a fire (Wands). The result is burnout. Likewise, too much rationalization saps the will.

PAGE OF CUPS

Air of Water | intellectualized emotion | study

Affirmation: Deep understanding of the emotions I feel allows me to communicate them verbally.

This Page, flushed from the success of his journey through the Cups, applies intelligence to emotion. His feelings are logically ordered and his relationships are healthy. He is fascinated by this, and so he absorbs himself in philosophical discussion and psychological study. His curiosity expands into a study of the nature of everything.

APPEARANCE IN A SPREAD

The Page of Cups is a studious soul. His appearance in a reading represents sound advice to examine a situation more thoroughly, to consider going back to school, to take a workshop, or somehow to increase your knowledge.

REVERSED MEANING

Reversed, too much Air on Water leads to choppy seas and, if the conditions are right, a devastating hurricane of emotions. Don't take the whirlwind too seriously. The emotions you are feeling now will change.

PAGE OF SWORDS

Air of Air | rationalization | secret

Affirmation: I can help others without any need of acknowledgement.

The Page of Swords is ever so slightly sneaky. He acts in the background, with all good intent, but preferring to remain unseen. He deals with difficult decisions by resolving them in secret. He understands both sides of the equation and can live undetected on either side of the fence, like a spy or secret agent.

APPEARANCE IN A SPREAD

Life seems to go that much easier when this Page is around. When he appears you can be assured there's someone there to help things go your way, without you knowing anything about it. He ensures a smooth path by planning ahead for several contingencies.

Do a little detective work to find out who it is you should be thanking for their selflessness.

REVERSED MEANING

The reverse of this card indicates that someone is spying or acting secretly for inappropriate, selfish reasons. This Page in reverse springs a surprise on you completely out of the blue, and then expects endless praise and accolades.

PAGE OF COINS

Air of Earth | intellectualized centre | focus

Affirmation: I focus on the here and now.

This Page is easily distracted, and has a tendency to miss the wood for the trees. His message is to step back and look at the big picture. Do you ever get the sense that all you are doing is flitting from one thing to the next? The Page of Coins embodies a reminder to gather your energy and maintain focus.

APPEARANCE IN A SPREAD

In a relationship reading, this Page would be the lover you once swore you'd never have anything to do with, until they proved to be attentive and attuned to you. In the bedroom, this Page makes your head spin. But can you trust them? When you are with them you don't doubt they are your perfect match, yet when you are apart the questions creep back in.

REVERSED MEANING

Too much Air on Earth can create a sandstorm or tornado. A reversed Page suggests that you need to concentrate on the practical details. It also urges you to be sensible about your finances – don't just wish for the coins to appear.

EXERCISE

Take the court card pile and shuffle it. Then ask yourself the following questions and use the court cards to answer them.

- **CARD 1** Who am I today?
- **CARD 2** Who do I need to be today?
- **CARD 3** Who will help me today?
- **CARD 4** Who will hinder me today?
- **CARD 5** Who am I in relation to this project (situation, endeavour, relationship, etc.)?
- **CARD 6** Who will I be at the conclusion of this project?

Keep notes in your tarot journal of the questions asked, the cards drawn, your initial interpretation and your realizations as the day went on.

EXAMPLE READING

CARD 1 Queen of Coins

CARD 2 King of Coins

These two cards show a clear progression from the Queen to the King of Coins, the suit that pertains to health, money and tangible things. The draw tells me I need to abandon the emotional stance symbolized by the Queen and take a more centred approach in these earthly areas. In whatever situations I have to deal with today, I should step up a gear and be adept as the King, rather than secure as the Queen.

If the cards had been different and my second card was the Page of Coins, the tarot would be telling me that I need to adopt a questioning or flexible viewpoint, as relating to some health, financial or physical issue.

Knight

also known as Prince, Brother or Son

Consider the progression through the courts as though, having taken the journey of the pips, you now think about it (Page), act on it (Knight), feel it fully (Queen) and finally become it (King). The second stage of assimilation or realization after the journey through the suit is that of action and will. This concept is traditionally conveyed in the tarot with a Knight astride a horse. Modern decks preserve the masculine energies of action, pride in accomplishment, leadership and so forth, but rename the bearer of these energies Prince, Brother or Son.

In a reading a Knight can indicate a young man (or woman), a necessary action, a forewarning of an action another person will take, or an aspect of your will that needs work. In elemental analysis, Wands and Swords are seen as masculine and Cups and Coins are seen as feminine. The traditional order of the suits makes for two masculine/ feminine pairs, thus: Wands/Cups and Swords/Coins. The Knights in each pairing are almost diametrically opposed in terms of both meaning and action. The Knight of Wands is leaving while Cups is staying; Swords is charging ahead recklessly while Coins is taking his time and acting slowly and carefully.

Like the hot high noon in summer, the fiery, wilful Knights may go overboard with passion and vigour, which sometimes leads to mistakes, but their intention is always noble and earnest, and they accept correction with good grace. They are eager to learn and do whatever is right. They get things done.

KNIGHT OF WANDS

Fire of Fire | wilful | departure

Affirmation: I can leave any time I choose.

Being around the Knight of Wands is always an exciting and passionate experience. Never afraid to try something new, he may never settle down. In work, this Knight is a powerful force who pushes ahead any plan he is involved in, though the project languishes when he moves on to the next. In relationships, he loves passionately and leaves silently.

APPEARANCE IN A SPREAD

This Knight is a thrill seeker who enjoys skydiving, fast cars and all other forms of excitement. He seeks out opportunities to perform great deeds, put wrongs to right, or simply to display his prowess. When this card appears, you are being called to action. The Knight must be able to point to something and say 'I did that.'

REVERSED MEANING

You've reached burnout or stagnation. The Knight tells you to depart but, unfortunately, your path is blocked or you don't know in which direction to turn. Like the ashes left after the fire, you may feel very small and helpless, as though blown about by the winds of fate.

KNIGHT OF CUPS

Fire of Water | passionate emotion | proposal

Affirmation: I share the beauty of my life with others.

This Knight is on fire with his feelings of love, passion, righteousness and whatever other emotions capture his heart. He takes his feelings very seriously. He sincerely believes they will last for ever. As such, he acts on them without debate, putting aside the deliberation he favoured as the Page.

APPEARANCE IN A SPREAD

This card often comes up when the question asked relates to a marriage proposal, or else it may suggest an invitation to join forces with another person. This is the Knight in Shining Armour who whisks you off into the sunset on his horse. He also uses the Cup to toast an occasion, celebrate, break the ice and soothe any uncomfortable feelings.

REVERSED MEANING

Reversed, the Knight tells you that those passionate feelings have lost their fervour. He isn't bringing a favourable invitation or proposal this time, or maybe now is not a good time to accept one.

KNIGHT OF SWORDS

Fire of Air | passionate intellect | charge

Affirmation: I realize my wildest dreams by acting on my great ideas.

This Knight is on fire with his ideas, beliefs and goals. After the very difficult journey of the Swords suit that ended with depression and so much backstabbing, this Knight acts in a way to protect himself from any such future despair. He claws his way up from the bottom. He uses the sword of intellect to defeat others in the name of truth and justice and is the man to turn to if you truly want the job done.

APPEARANCE IN A SPREAD

When this card appears, you know you have to stop sitting on the fence pondering and take charge of a situation. It may also mean that someone with take charge qualities will help or lead you.

REVERSED MEANING

Reversed, this Knight means that the sharp intellect has grown dull, or is clouded by greed or some other negative emotion. You have grown weary of the everlasting fight against evil and are experiencing despair. Try to remember the intellectual reasons for your struggles and efforts.

KNIGHT OF COINS

Fire of Earth | passionate centre | caution

Affirmation: I am very careful with my resources.

Emerging from the journey of his suit at a place of reward and permanence, the Knight of Coins is the most cautious and circumspect of the Knights. His viewpoint is more balanced than that of the Page; he is able to see the detail as well as the long-term goal. This Knight realizes that if he wants to achieve his goals he needs to be thrifty with his time, energy and money. His actions almost always yield successful results because he is so careful in the planning and execution.

APPEARANCE IN A SPREAD

This card tells the querent to proceed with great care, especially in financial matters. Keep an eye on the detail and be cautious in the planning and execution of any project.

REVERSED MEANING

Too much Fire on Earth leads to the bad smell of waste and inefficiency. This upside-down Knight tells you that you are being overcautious. You will never enjoy the fruits of your frugality, although you're heaping them up in great piles.

EXERCISE

Here's a fun way to look back at your life and understand more about who you were in the past and how you have become who you are now. It will give you a fresh perspective on personal history long past.

- Look back over the accomplishments of your life, good and bad, things that you remember fondly or with chagrin. Make a chronological list. Likely milestones may include:
  - Break-up of my first romance
  - Getting my college degree
  - A trip or other adventure
  - Marriage
  - Big pay rise or promotion
  - Leaving a job
  - Having children
  - Losing a loved one
  - Winning a prize
- Shuffle the court cards and draw one for each milestone. Use it to understand who you were at that time in your life and note the changes in terms of the tarot. Did you progress from Page to King? Did you change from Fire to Water, passion to emotion?
- Now take the pip cards, shuffle them and deal out one for each milestone to explain why you were that court card and what energy you were working through at that point in your life.

EXAMPLE READING

CARD 1 Knight of Cups

The milestone in question was a trip to India. At that time in my life I was offered a marriage proposal and was struggling with how best to get out of it. I've always been an idealist, like this Knight is, and I just couldn't settle for a marriage without love. I remember putting the whole thing on hold and escaping to India for a month so that I could do some deep soul-searching.

CARD 2 6 of Wands (reversed)

The 6 of Wands reversed represents the bad news that surrounded me at the time. It was these negatives that came together to push me out of the situation and into a much happier, more satisfying life path. So, even though I remember the stress and angst of that trip, the energy surrounding me at that point was one of victory. Six months later these energies were fully manifested in a new job, a peaceful house, and lots of great interests and activities.

Queen

also known as Mother, Birth Giver or Nurturer

The Queens and Kings are the rulers of their suit. In traditional decks and most modern decks, they sit on thrones, wearing crowns and elaborate regalia. The Queen is the mother figure, the feminine side of authority, the nurturer you turn to for comfort and emotional support. She presides over social and family issues, healthcare and education.

I'm referring to the Queen as 'she', but the Queen card can refer to the querent even if male, or a man in the querent's life. Similarly, the Kings can refer to a female in a reading, though I will refer to 'he' and 'his' when describing their characters. It's the traits of personality and character that are important, not gender.

The Queen is an emotional assimilation of the journey from Ace to 10. This maternal, nurturing figure reflects on the day's events as the sun sets over a western lake on a cool autumn day. She recalls the full spectrum of feelings experienced on her suit's journey. Being thus fully experienced in emotions, she is no longer emotionally disturbed by life's reverses. She always remembers the joys and triumphs, and proceeds through life with a deep sense of satisfaction that exerts a favourable influence on all around her. Her strength is love.

QUEEN OF WANDS

Water of Earth | emotional will | friend

Affirmation: Today I am my own best friend.

When you apply emotion to will you become the staunchest friend, the kind who sticks fast through thick and thin and everything in between. The Queen of Wands may not be your best friend, or the friend you go out and do everything with, but when you need her she's there and always will be. She always listens and she dispenses sound, friendly advice. She may be quirky, but that's her free spirit and unchained will expressing themselves as exuberant eccentricity. You probably wouldn't want to be the Queen of Wands, but you are really glad to have her on your side.

APPEARANCE IN A SPREAD

This card tells you to expect friendship. Maybe a friend you haven't heard from for a while is going to give you a call. Or maybe you need to go and be a friend to someone else.

REVERSED MEANING

Reversed, this card would indicate that you have an issue with a friend, or with friendship in general. Ask yourself if you are being the best friend you can be. Maybe one of your friends needs you now.

QUEEN OF CUPS

Water of Water | emotional strength | parent

Affirmation: I can parent my inner child.

The Queen of Cups is the quintessential 'mummy' card. She is the absolute best person to have around when you need some tender care. She's the kind mother who brings you a tray when you are sick in bed, who takes you to all sorts of classes, events and shows. She's the one who nurtures your growth in every way.

APPEARANCE IN A SPREAD

The Queen of your heart card can indicate a fortunate relationship. In fact, any Cups court card is a good omen for romance and positive emotions. The card points to someone you like and with whom you find communication easy. You become this Queen when you truly love and accept yourself just the way you are.

REVERSED MEANING

The other way up, the Queen signifies someone who may not be suited to parenthood or the responsibility of dependants (like pets, for example). It signals a lack of emotional strength.

QUEEN OF SWORDS

Water of Air | emotional intellect | independence

Affirmation: I deal with anything that comes my way with efficiency.

The Queen of Swords is the widow of the deck. She is strong because she has to be. Some perceive her as cold and stubborn, but it's on her shoulders that all the decisions and responsibilities of running the kingdom fall when the King is not present. She is seen as cruel and insensitive, when actually she feels very deeply. However, she does not let her emotions affect her decision making. This Queen steps in to save the day when others prove unreliable.

APPEARANCE IN A SPREAD

This card bodes ill for romantic relationships. Your husband or partner may well be about to disappoint you. Expect to exercise your independence. Sometimes you can only rely on yourself.

REVERSED MEANING

Reversed, this Queen can indicate a lack of grieving: that you have not allowed yourself to feel unpleasant but necessary feelings. It also warns you to watch out for intelligence acting without regard to emotion and the feelings of self and others.

QUEEN OF COINS

Water of Earth | emotional centre | security

Affirmation: I have what I need to feel secure.

This lucky Queen has a secure job, marriage, house, life insurance, good pension scheme, etc. From an earthly standpoint, life looks rosy. She's a good sign for business and financial success, indicating that a given situation will work out in the end. This lady really has her life in order. Nothing rocks or shakes her. She is the stable centre of her family and group of friends.

APPEARANCE IN A SPREAD

Sadly, this card often comes up to indicate a married man when a female querent is asking about a love interest. The card reveals that he is secure in his marriage and just wants a little action on the side. He's not going to leave his wife for the querent.

REVERSED MEANING

The Queen of Coins in reverse can bring insecurities to light. Perhaps you are due a check on your physical and financial security. Whatever the nature of the unease, the card tells you to root it out and deal with it.

EXERCISE

This five-card 'Queen for the Day' exercise poses five questions. Using the 16 court cards only, shuffle, cut and lay out five cards with the following questions in mind:

- **CARD 1** How do I nurture myself?
- **CARD 2** Who nurtures me?
- **CARD 3** What nurtures me?
- **CARD 4** What do I need to support and nurture my bank account (or another concern)?
- **CARD 5** How do I get it?

EXAMPLE READING

CARD 1 PAGE OF CUPS

This initial draw tells me to nurture myself with more study. I need to look more deeply into what interests and amuses me. Reading for entertainment comes to mind as a great way to nurture myself and feed my brain. Or perhaps I could take swimming lessons and actually learn to do the strokes properly.

CARD 2 QUEEN OF WANDS

A friend nurtures me. I give her a ring and set a lunch date. (Over time, court cards will come to represent specific people to you.)

CARD 3 KNIGHT OF CUPS (REVERSED)

The Knight of Cups reversed is my true introvert personality showing itself. Not accepting invitations and avoiding some social interactions are decisions that nurture me. Spending time with others, while enjoyable, can be exhausting.

CARD 4 PAGE OF WANDS (REVERSED)

Asked about my bank account, the reversed Page of Wands points out a lack of faith I have in my own ability to manage my finances. It challenges me to trust in myself, my willpower and my financial plans that the money will come through.

CARD 5 QUEEN OF CUPS (REVERSED)

The Queen of Cups tells me that the way to support myself over the bank account problem is to avoid getting overemotional about it. I should stop worrying. On the practical level, I need to stop taking on dependants and new financial responsibilities (and stop shopping!).

King

also known as Protector, Ruler, Provider or Father

Finally, we come to the solid maturity of the King, replete with the wisdom accumulated along his suit's journey. He is representative of the best and highest of his element. The King traditionally deals with issues of security, economics, foreign policy and disaster relief. He bears ultimate responsibility for everything that happens in his kingdom, even down to weather and disease.

King energy is stable and centred; it isn't easily moved or swayed. His power is grounded in practicality and the wisdom of experience. When you reach the King, life's lessons have been fully assimilated and are put into practice. His throne is a comfortable resting place that has been earned.

It's where he sits to listen to his subjects. Reversed tarot Kings sit smugly, even arrogantly, in ivory towers, far removed from the reality experienced by their citizens or dependants, whom they often neglect in the interest of more self-indulgent pursuits.

Like the cold depths of midnight under a mountain in winter, the Kings are grounded, determined and firmly set in their wise ways. Rightfully proud of their accomplishments and power, they issue orders and devise rules for their suits. They are what every card preceding them aspires to become.

RE DI DANARI

KING OF WANDS

Earth of Fire | centred will | honesty

Affirmation: My word is true.

The King of Wands has integrity. He prompts you to be honest with yourself and everyone else. He can be trusted to keep his word and to do what he says he will. He makes you believe in yourself. You wouldn't dare let him down because he has such strong faith in you. He can be trusted to speak his mind and firmly believe in what he says.

APPEARANCE IN A SPREAD

This card usually points to the presence or influence of a man with practical skills, like a lumberjack or a handyman with a garage full of power tools. Whoever he is, he is his own boss and is probably bossy by nature.

REVERSED MEANING

Reversed, this man may mean well, but he never quite keeps his word and can't be depended on. He's the person who always cancels at the last minute, leaving you in the lurch. This draw can also imply shoddy workmanship.

KING OF CUPS

Earth of Water | centred emotion | mate

Affirmation: I love.

The King of Cups is in touch with and understands his feelings, and is able to verbalize and discuss them. He is easy to be around. You feel good when he's in the same room. He may be musical or artistic, even comedic; he is interesting, perhaps fascinating. His profession involves helping others. He's always willing to help and willing to listen.

APPEARANCE IN A SPREAD

The King of your heart, this card is a very auspicious sign for a mate and long-term relationship. You have an excellent chance of finding romance and love.

REVERSED MEANING

This person may be too in touch with his feelings, to the exclusion of yours. A reversed King of Cups tells you he's a bit selfish and self-absorbed. He isn't the ideal mate, although he has potential. Think in terms of friendship, partnership, etc., not in terms of marriage.

KING OF SWORDS

Earth of Air | centred intellect | ethics

Affirmation: Today I will make the best choices I can.

This King is the ultimate intellectual and has a ruthless ability to reach difficult decisions by apportioning blame, punishment and even redundancies. He takes full personal responsibility for the results of his decisions. He has a deep commitment to his ethical standards and moral beliefs, and is willing to explain and debate them.

APPEARANCE IN A SPREAD

This card can be a sign that you face an ethical or moral dilemma. A decision must be made; making no decision would mean failure and loss. It can also indicate a brilliant intellect.

REVERSED MEANING

Reversed, the Swords King suggests that the best decision has not been made. The card also implies a faulty line of reasoning, or that emotions are completely divorced from intellect. This King appears cool, but in reality he simply isn't in touch with his emotions. He can't verbalize what he is feeling and sometimes he pretends he doesn't feel, so his emotions explode as anger and irritation with those around him.

KING OF COINS

Earth of Earth | grounded | adept

Affirmation: I am that good!

This King has surpassed the stage of mastery. He has the Midas touch: everything he touches becomes successful and prosperous. He is truly passionate about his endeavours. He may or may not have a lot of money (he will if making money is his passion), but he's got an awful lot to show for his efforts. He is talented and very good at what he does. This King deserves appreciation.

APPEARANCE IN A SPREAD

In a relationship reading, this King indicates a good mate if financial security and a nice house are important to you. He may not talk much about his feelings, but he will share both his work and his accomplishments with you.

REVERSED MEANING

Reversed, the King says you have failed to become adept in the situation under question. Your Midas touch has become tarnished. You may be spending more than you are making. Hopes for success probably won't be realized without considerable effort or a change in tactics.

EXERCISE

This four-card exercise will help you give yourself the approval and recognition you need to endorse yourself as ruler of your own destiny.

- Pick a card from the deck that describes the situation in which you want to rule and become King (card 1).
- Ask yourself what type of King you want to become.
- Shuffle and cut the court cards only. Pull cards until you get a King to answer (card 2).
- Ask yourself what it will take to make you a King of this situation.
- Shuffle and cut the pips and majors separately and pull one card from each pile to find your answer (cards 3 and 4).

EXAMPLE READING

CARD 1 10 OF COINS

To illustrate the King exercise let's use a reading I carried out for a woman who came to me desperate to gain control over her chaotic household. We began by choosing the 10 of Coins to represent her house.

CARD 2 KING OF COINS

The seventh card we turned up was the King of Coins, the same suit as the card that described the querent's problem. This King told us that, in order to gain control over her house, my client needed to become adept. She must fully own, honour her house and tend to its maintenance and upkeep. She should make her house her passion and her life, at least temporarily.

CARD 3 8 OF SWORDS

The querent's pip card was the 8 of Swords, which implied that the way to go about gaining control of her house was to restrict herself to it. She was always at work, shopping or socializing, so it's no wonder the scene at home was out of control.

CARD 4 0 THE FOOL

Whenever the Fool appears in a reading, the querent should ask 'What is the foolish choice? What is the risky thing I dare not do?' The querent's answer in this case was 'Run a business from home.' She had been afraid that running a business from home would add to the chaos, but her cards revealed that, on the contrary, working from home would force her to become more organized and adept at managing her house.

Part Two
Using the Tarot for Positive Change

✠

The previous chapters gave an overview of the 78 tarot cards and how to perform basic tarot readings.

Part 2 explains in more detail how to use the tarot as a tool for life planning. I explain what spreads you need to use, how to frame your questions, and then how to interpret, understand and use the answers given by the tarot to bring about positive change in your life.

We begin by looking at the present as a building block for the future. Award yourself the time to get to know yourself better. You are worth it! You may be surprised at some of the discoveries you make simply because you never gave yourself the space to think. As you get to know yourself better, you will become more and more successful at life planning with the tarot.

Framing the Question

The most powerful way to use tarot cards for positive change is to ask empowering questions. Frame your questions in such a way that they will lead to solutions and helpful answers.

✠

CONSIDER THE QUESTION: IS MY LOVER CHEATING ON ME?

By its nature, the positive answer to this question is a negative: 'No, my lover is not cheating on me.' The negative answer is a positive: 'Yes, my lover is cheating on me.' It takes an extremely experienced card reader to answer such a question definitively, and, even if accurate, where's the proof, one way or another? Is knowing the answer to this question really going to be useful? What will you do with the information – confront your lover with the tarot cards? A better way to frame the question is: What do I need to know about my lover?

Staying Focused

The cards that come up in your reading may or may not have anything to do with the relationship, but they will reveal what you need to know. Consider, too, that it isn't strictly ethical to snoop on anyone without their permission or knowledge, even metaphysically with tarot cards. The most constructive questions are those that concern you, the person you can actively improve, such as:

- Why don't I trust my partner?
- Is this relationship right for me?
- How can I improve the communication in this relationship?
- What do I need to do so that my partner can trust me with the truth?

Working on you, becoming the person you want to be, will lead to tremendous results in terms of personal growth, personal power and your happiness.

Allow yourself the space and time to work with the tarot in a calm environment where you will be free from distraction and interruption. You deserve that time and space to access your own intuition and inner knowledge. A flat table with good lighting is essential. I like a velvet or thick cloth covering so that I can pick up the cards easily. Candles, aromas, beautiful music – use whatever helps you relax and focus on the cards and yourself.

chapter three

Your Present and Future Life

No one can tell you what to do with your life unless you surrender your power and allow it. These tarot spreads show you how to reclaim your ability to guide and direct your own life. You have all the power and knowledge you need within you. You were born with it. You still have it. The tarot helps you to see it with your external, physical eyes so that you can more easily claim it and put it to use.

Where Are You Now?

First, you need to get a clear idea of what's going on in your life right now and how this came to be. The process will require honesty on your part and some examination of the past. It's known as the 'mirror phase' of tarot life planning, where you use the tarot like a mirror to see the self clearly, and to see what is behind the self, its composition. It's vital you understand where you are now and where you are heading before you decide to make any changes.

Life Planning with Tarot

We then move on to look at many example layouts, with a view to learning to create your own. As you embark on the process of life planning it makes sense to start with the smaller layouts. You can use these as building blocks to understand larger, more complex spreads. Spend plenty of time with individual cards by studying them and meditating on their meaning. You can use any tarot deck that feels right to you, or that you find attractive.

You can sit anywhere in your house or create a special tarot reading space with incense, candles and chimes. You can shuffle the cards however you like.

Am I Asking the Right Questions?

The most important choices you will make when reading the tarot are what questions to ask. We find ourselves frustrated with the people and events in our lives because we cannot control or change them. All we can control or change is our very own self. Because of this, it makes sense to concentrate the question on the self. You can ask questions about motivations and causes, but it should always be done with a view to self-improvement, self-transformation and self-manifestation. The tarot lends itself very well to these sorts of questions and this sort of attitude. It doesn't lend itself to frivolous questions that result in ridiculous or confusing answers.

Some tarot readers even ask the tarot if they have chosen the proper question, or if the reading will be successful, before ever attempting the actual reading. For example, you might pick a question, then shuffle the deck and draw one card to help you to decide whether to proceed. If the selected card is upright, the tarot is telling you that you have chosen the right question. You then put that card back in the deck and shuffle and lay out the cards for your question. If the selected card is reversed, on the other hand, you need to reconsider the question and reframe its language before going ahead with the reading, or even put the cards away and try again at a later time.

Positive Change Means:

breathing more easily | being happier | living more freely | resting peacefully | speaking truthfully | eating healthily | working gainfully | loving every moment of the day.

Your Life Now

Ask the tarot about who you are in the present and the cards will reflect the life you currently choose to live. Any of the following spreads can help you understand better how you live from day to day and who you are. If you are at the cusp of major change and growth in your life, use only the major arcana to clarify the significant energies you face.

THE QUESTION: Who am I?

CARD LAYOUT: Shuffle and lay out the cards in the numbered order shown.

 1

BODY The card that appears in the Body position of this spread tells you something about your physical body, such as its state of health or why you have the body that you do. The card can also relate to where your body lives, what it touches and what work it does; this position represents all things physical and tangible.

 2

MIND The Mind card concerns your mental body, your intellectual powers and why you have them. It can help explain the reasons why you think the way you do, your thinking process and the conclusions you have decided upon. Open your mind to the message in this card.

 3

SPIRIT The Spirit card highlights the state of your soul, your spiritual life or your relationship with the divine. It can reveal your progress in fulfilling your life's higher purpose. Used as a verb, 'divine' means to understand by intuition. Open your spirit to divine the nature of your own divinity.

THE QUESTION: Where am I?

1. PATH

The first card reveals exactly what aspect of your life's journey is under discussion. If the meaning doesn't strike you immediately, use the number and suit of the card to decipher your path. Smaller numbers refer to something you've recently begun. As you gain skill and practise with the tarot, you can choose this card yourself to describe a chosen path, and then pick the second card to assess how far you've travelled.

1   **2**

2. PROGRESS

The second card is a progress indicator. If the number of this card is higher than that of the first card, you are moving forward. If the number is lower, you might be moving back or repeating a lesson in some way. If the suit is the same, you are staying on track. If the suit is different, you should ask yourself what has changed about your path recently, and why. What does this say about you and your path?

THE QUESTION: **What are my strengths and weaknesses?**

STRENGTHS (LEFT COLUMN)

These cards represent your strengths. Examine them one by one and consider the ways in which each indicates one of your strengths. Do the cards that you have drawn seem correct? You may be surprised by what the cards reveal. Consider why this is.

1

2

3

1

2

3

WEAKNESSES (RIGHT COLUMN)

Examine the cards that reveal your weaknesses in the same way. Look for repetition and patterns in number, suit and symbols. You may find that all your weaknesses belong to one suit or energy, or are all one number. Think about what this signifies. What are the cards trying to tell you?

THE QUESTION: **What influences affect my life?**

1

2

3

4

5

6

INFLUENCE OF OTHERS

Start by thinking about the influence that other people have on you. Then examine the cards. Do they confirm your thoughts? They may add fresh insight.

MY INFLUENCE

Now think about the ways in which you influence other people. What do the cards in this bottom row tell you about this?

Where You Are

This tarot layout reveals the progress you've made in various areas of your life. Choose from intellectual growth, career advancement, wisdom, spiritual path, your current romantic relationship, friendships, parent–child relationships, health or any another area that concerns you. In a relationship layout, the two cards that you choose – known as 'significators' – represent the two people in the relationship. In an alternative spread relating to your personal path, the first card could describe you now and the second describe your goal or aspiration.

THE QUESTION: Where am I in this relationship?

CARD LAYOUT: Choose an appropriate significator for yourself and another for the other person in the relationship. Set these two cards aside. Shuffle and cut the deck as you prefer and pull off the top seven cards without turning them over. Add the two significator cards to these seven cards. Shuffle a few times and lay out all nine cards in a simple line, left to right.

EXAMPLE READING

Jennifer wants to get back together with her ex-partner. Although the relationship has ended, the couple continue to work at the same law firm and have found they have a good working relationship.

			SIGNIFICATOR
			(JENNIFER'S PARTNER)
10 OF SWORDS	KING OF COINS	THE EMPRESS	KING OF CUPS

The cards to the left of your significator show the stages you have passed through to get where you are now.

IMMEDIATE IMPRESSIONS

This type of card layout can be read in many different ways, but the best way to understand it is to focus on the position of the cards surrounding each significator.

What really leaps out is the appearance of the Empress next to the King of Cups and the Emperor next to the Queen of Cups. This implies that both Jennifer and her partner are going to have to extend themselves for this relationship to work. They have somehow confined themselves to lesser roles whereas they could achieve much more.

Both 6s fall between the King and Queen of Cups, which speaks of a need for resolution in intellectual and power issues between Jennifer and her partner. There are three Swords cards, whereas the only Cups cards are the ones pre-chosen for the spread as significators. Struggle and intellectualization are heavily present in this relationship. Absent are romance and simple affection.

SUMMARY

The fact that the Queen of Cups has come up nearly last indicates that Jennifer has advanced through all the pictured energies and stages (including two Kings, an Empress and a Knight!) to get to where she is. From this point her goal is toward owning and embracing ultimate authority in her own life and, more specifically, in her love life. The cards between the significators indicate delayed change, charging ahead, and good news or victory. The slightest catalyst could send these two into each other's arms.

SIGNIFICATOR
(JENNIFER)

6 OF SWORDS	KNIGHT OF SWORDS	6 OF WANDS	QUEEN OF CUPS	THE EMPEROR

The cards between the two significators show what stands between you; what the two of you have yet to overcome or accomplish, or the tasks before the pair of you.

The cards to the right show where your current path is taking you. Interpret the cards to the left and right of the other significator in the same way.

Why You Are
The Way You Are

Let's examine some of the aspects of your personality and consider why you are that way. You might want to put the spotlight on your sociability, for example, or stress quotient, your ability to think critically, your mental outlook, or how you relate to others in work, play, romance or as a supervisor/subordinate. Choose one aspect or choose many.

THE QUESTION: What is my social nature?

CARD LAYOUT: Decide which aspect of yourself you would like to examine. Shuffle and cut the deck as you prefer. Pull two cards and place them side by side.

EXAMPLE READING

In these first two pairs I'm pulling cards for sociability, assuming with the first draw that I am an introvert, and with the second that I am an extrovert. Which are you? Or are you part one and part the other, depending on the circumstance?

MY QUALITY

WHY I HAVE IT

THE MOON (REVERSED)

The Moon reversed indicates a bright light and someone who shines at night or when things are still and silent. This is the true introvert's nature; it is not an illusion.

2 OF COINS

The reason why I am introverted, is that I am juggling two things, or too many things, and struggling to find the right balance. It may be that I can't find balance unless in small or one-on-one situations because I become easily distracted by the simultaneous presence of many viewpoints.

KNIGHT OF CUPS

You won't find a greater extrovert than the Knight of Cups. Like the hospitable Knight, I am always extending invitations to lunch, coffee or other get-togethers.

QUEEN OF WANDS

The reason I am like this, as shown by the Queen, is my steadfast, friendly nature. I seek out others because I enjoy being a friend as much as having a friend.

THE QUESTION: What is the nature of my role at work?

EXAMPLE READING

At work we often have roles both as a supervisor and a subordinate, even if we only supervise our own work or customers. Joseph is very unhappy in his job as a salesman. The first card pair explores his role as a supervisor, and the second pair his role as a subordinate.

MY ROLE

2 OF SWORDS (REVERSED)

This card indicates that Joseph is even-minded and easily makes decisions in his role as a supervisor over his clients. He can't do any more than his company allows and thus feels intellectually stymied.

ITS NATURE

2 OF CUPS (REVERSED)

Joseph feels like a company yes-man because he's not able to partner his clients in a meaningful way. He builds up a good relationship with them in the lead up to a sale, but then never sees the client again.

ACE OF COINS

The Coins suit confirms that Joseph is making money for the company. However, the fact that it is an Ace rather than a 3 or 8 suggests that his achievements are modest.

THE TOWER

The Tower reveals the fact that Joseph plans to bring about some upheaval by leaving as soon as possible. The reason he is biding his time and doing the minimum is because, as soon as he can, he'll be changing employers.

Planning for the Future

Now let's look at your future; not your destiny, but the happiest future of your wildest dreams. Where would you like to be in a year's time? How about five years from now? Take a flight of fancy and imagine the possibilities.

THE QUESTION: Where do I truly want to be in a year's time?

CARD LAYOUT: Shuffle and cut the cards as you prefer. Draw one card. If it's a positive card that resonates with a cherished dream, pull the next card to find out how you can stay on course throughout the year. If it's a negative card that reflects something you do not desire, pull the next card to find out how to accept and understand this.

EXAMPLE READING

In these spreads I'm looking for advice on where I'm going in my life and how I should get there.

WHAT IS MY DREAM?

PAGE OF COINS

The Page of Coins can be read as a message to shift focus, so my dream card could represent a change in position, like becoming a manager with responsibility for the goals of the entire company rather than the portion of it I deal with at present.

HOW DO I ACHIEVE/ ACCEPT THIS?

QUEEN OF WANDS

Assuming that becoming a manager, as suggested by the first card, is something I dream of doing, the Queen of Wands as my second draw would tell me to stay on course with this ambition by cultivating some friends within the company.

However, if the idea of becoming a manager doesn't resonate with me in any meaningful way, I should read this card in terms of acceptance of this fact. In this case, the Queen of Wands reminds me to be my own best friend and also to rely on those I consider my friends. One of these friends may be able to offer some useful advice about where I should go from here.

REG. DI BASTONI

FAN. DI DANARI

THE QUESTION: Where do I truly want to be in five years' time?

CARD LAYOUT: Shuffle and cut the cards as you prefer. Draw five cards.

WHAT DO I WANT TO ACHIEVE?

6 OF COINS

The 6 of Coins is about having enough money to share and give away; being in a position to do a lot of things that I've always wanted. It's easy to understand that I desire this for myself in five years' time.

WHO DO I WANT TO BE?

KING OF WANDS

The King of Wands also makes perfect sense. This is a card of great personal power. It is confirmation of wanting to run my own business.

WHAT DO I WANT TO CONQUER?

3 OF SWORDS

This card indicates growth and expansion born of sorrow. In five years' time, I shall have dealt with many heartaches, large and small.

WHAT DO I NEED TO KNOW?

3 OF CUPS

This 3 tells me there is joy to be found in widening my social circle. Social contacts can turn into business opportunities. Personal recommendation is the best type of reference.

WHAT DO I NEED TO DO?

3 OF WANDS

Three 3s indicate plenty of growth and expansion here. The Wands and Cups represent treasures to be found through exploration of many new paths, and that there is joy to be found in expanding social connections.

SUMMARY

The message here is that if I truly want the benefits of the 6 of Coins and King of Wands, I will have to pass through the challenge of the 3 of Swords, and embrace it as eagerly as the pleasures of the 3 of Cups and 3 of Wands.

How to Achieve Your Dream Future

This layout is designed to display a progression of stages you will have to pass through to achieve your goals. It's generally assumed the steps appear in order, but that might not always be so. When you carry out the exercise, remember that the future is not set in stone. It can change because you have free will.

THE QUESTION: What steps should I take to achieve my dream future?

CARD LAYOUT: Shuffle and cut your deck in the way you prefer. On the basis of the tarot work you've already done, choose one card that describes where you are now.

Lay it to the lower left of your workspace.

Choose one card that describes where you want to be and lay it to the upper right of your workspace. Ask the universe to show you your path between these two as you shuffle the deck. Draw five cards and place them in an ascending ladder across your workspace, from left to right.

EXAMPLE READING

I am just starting out working for myself, trusting my own intuition over conventional wisdom, and ask the cards how best to achieve my goal of becoming fully self-employed and my own boss.

1

2

3

4

5

6

7

IMMEDIATE IMPRESSIONS

The four major arcana cards indicate that my right path is a difficult one, involving some major life changes.

The Devil and Death can be awkward energies to accept and work with. Their appearance tends to make the heart skip!

1 WHERE I AM NOW: Ace of Wands

2 STEP 1: 0 The Fool (reversed)

The Fool's appearance reversed tells me to stick with what I know and not to run headlong into a new adventure. Risk should be minimized.

3 STEP 2: 15 The Devil

The Devil warns of danger and self-deception. It's my wake-up call, bringing me back down to earth. This card warns me to be alert to self-defeating behaviour.

4 STEP 3: 9 The Hermit (reversed)

The Hermit reversed advises me to hold off on my tendency to withdraw and be introspective. At the moment it would be more appropriate to look outward and to others for knowledge and wisdom.

5 STEP 4: 4 of Swords

The 4 of Swords tells me to slow down and rest. I should schedule some downtime to recuperate, but only after I've acted on the lessons of the previous cards.

6 STEP 5: 13 Death (reversed)

Finally, the reversed Death card warns me of an ending to be avoided or delayed. It could be a warning that I will experience discouragement and give up just as I near my goal. In other words, 'Don't stop!'

7 WHERE I WANT TO BE: King of Wands

SUMMARY

Self-employment is not an easy path for everyone. Sadly, many people fail. The message of the cards, which warn of a struggle, is an appropriate one.

What is Most Important to You and Why

Some things are important to all of us: family, having food to eat, comfortable shelter, and some kind of purpose in our lives. Other things are only important to some of us. You may not be able to get along without a weekly football game, while your friend feels life isn't worth living without the ballet. Power and fame, and the desire we may have for them, can also play a significant role in our lives.

THE QUESTION: **What is most important to me in my career and why?**

CARD LAYOUT: Make a list of several things you feel are important to your happiness and sense of completeness. Shuffle the deck and deal three cards to find three more things that are important to you. Add these to the bottom of your list. Put those three cards back into the deck, then shuffle with the clear intent of understanding what these things mean to you and why they are important to you. Lay out a row of cards corresponding to the items on your list. Lay out a second row underneath. Julie made a list of two things that are important to her – career and peer respect. To establish the last three items on Julie's list, we pulled three cards: King of Wands (reversed) – Authority in reverse: not being a big boss; 9 of Wands (reversed) – The reverse of continuity: variety; 13 Death – Eventual retirement.

EXAMPLE READING

For Julie, making a success of her career is imperative. Taking family and financial security as givens, she wants to concentrate completely on aspects of her job and career.

WHAT DOES THIS ASPECT OF MY CAREER MEAN TO ME?

CAREER	PEER RESPECT	NOT THE BOSS	VARIETY	RETIREMENT
THE MOON (REVERSED)	9 OF SWORDS	8 OF CUPS	ACE OF SWORDS	7 OF CUPS

WHY IS IT IMPORTANT?

CAREER	PEER RESPECT	NOT THE BOSS	VARIETY	RETIREMENT
2 OF COINS	10 OF WANDS	5 OF COINS	7 OF COINS	KING OF CUPS

IMMEDIATE IMPRESSIONS

The presence of lots of Cups and Coins indicates that Julie views her sense of emotional fulfilment combined with financial reward as particularly important markers of career success.

WHAT DOES THIS ASPECT OF MY CAREER MEAN TO ME?	WHY IS IT IMPORTANT?
CAREER THE MOON (REVERSED) This card symbolizes a negation of illusion. Julie has the sense that she is finally on track with her career.	**CAREER** 2 OF COINS Like a juggler, Julie's success is due to her ability to balance her spiritual beliefs and desires with her material career.
PEER RESPECT 9 OF SWORDS This 9 signifies anxiety. Julie sees the need for approval as a burden, and wishes it wasn't important to her as a measure of success.	**PEER RESPECT** 10 OF WANDS Having or not having the respect of her peers causes Julie significant stress, as this burdensome card indicates.
NOT THE BOSS 8 OF CUPS By avoiding a senior position, Julie is able to pick up and go as opportunity arises for her.	**NOT THE BOSS** 5 OF COINS She may need to leave if her position doesn't work out or a situation is lacking or unpleasant in some way.
VARIETY ACE OF SWORDS Variety for her means being able to act on new ideas.	**VARIETY** 7 OF COINS She can build on these ideas successfully because she is patient and has the know-how to bring her ideas to fruition over time.
RETIREMENT 7 OF CUPS Retirement means any number of imaginative things to her.	**RETIREMENT** KING OF CUPS The reason her horizons are so broad is that she expects to have reached emotional fulfilment.

SUMMARY

Julie has discovered three things about her career that are important but that she hasn't considered or verbalized before. The process also reveals what the different facets of her career mean to her and exactly why they are important. She is more worried about the opinions of others than she had realized, and so needs to develop a thicker skin and learn to be less needy of approval.

Mandala Layouts: The Path to Achieve True Happiness

In Buddhism, a mandala is a two-dimensional representation of a palace of meditation and possibility. Each object in the palace represents some aspect of wisdom or some important spiritual principle. Mandalas are commonly made from paper, cloth, rice flour and coloured sand. We are going to construct some mandalas using the tarot cards.

The Cardinal Mandala

CARD LAYOUT: Begin with the desire to achieve true happiness. As you shuffle the tarot deck, see the possible paths that lie before you now, and their end results. Lay out four cards, each headed in the four cardinal directions. South points toward you; North points away from you; East toward your right, West toward your left.

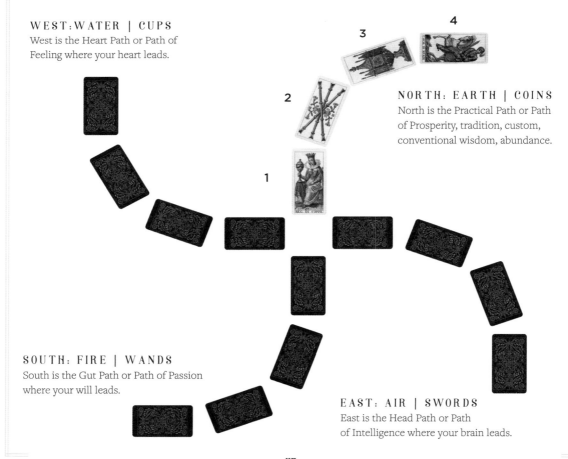

WEST:WATER | CUPS
West is the Heart Path or Path of Feeling where your heart leads.

NORTH: EARTH | COINS
North is the Practical Path or Path of Prosperity, tradition, custom, conventional wisdom, abundance.

SOUTH: FIRE | WANDS
South is the Gut Path or Path of Passion where your will leads.

EAST: AIR | SWORDS
East is the Head Path or Path of Intelligence where your brain leads.

THE QUESTION: Which path is best for me?

EXAMPLE READING

I performed a reading for the North Path of Prosperity to see how things would turn out if I were to follow this route. Whichever path you opt for, you can apply the questions below.

1 WHAT DOES THIS CHOICE OF DIRECTION MEAN TO ME?

QUEEN OF CUPS This first card tells me that, if I were to follow the Path of Prosperity, it would entail meeting the Queen of Cups, a lovely nurturing person who is fully in touch with her own emotions and who shares love with all those around her, or else I should become this Queen myself by helping and nurturing others.

2 WHAT GIFT WILL I RECEIVE FROM FOLLOWING THIS PATH?

3 OF WANDS In striving to become the stable, nurturing Queen I shall receive the gift of some unexpected treasure. I will expand my horizons and be able to accept something I can't even imagine right now, something very valuable that I do not have at present.

3 WHAT CHALLENGES WILL I FACE BY TRAVELLING THIS PATH?

ACE OF CUPS (REVERSED) The challenge I will face along this path could very well be a loss of a relationship, or a very quick end to a feeling or friendship (the reverse of a beginning). Or, by following this path, I will miss out on a relationship altogether.

4 WHAT IS THE FINAL RESULT OF FOLLOWING THIS PATH?

KNIGHT OF SWORDS Finally, the result of following the Path of Prosperity is that I shall learn to take control of my life and charge ahead and get things done – in the manner of a Knight. Note the significance of two Cups cards along the path. This emphasizes the importance of the heart in this reading.

Compass Mandala

The Compass mandala is very similar to the Cardinal mandala but it gives you eight choices of direction instead of four. Lay out as for the Cardinal mandala but add the following:

Northeast is the Path of Wisdom where your accumulated experience guides you | Northwest is the Path of Inspiration where you feel called to go | Southeast is the Path of Intuition where your subconscious leads | Southwest is the Path of Instinct the path that feels hardwired into your body.

CARD LAYOUT: Lay out the cards as if working a Compass mandala (see opposite), then lay out a second course of cards at a 30-degree angle to the others (Northeast, Northwest, Southeast, Southwest).

chapter four

Changing Your Physical Reality

Now that you have established a firm sense of who you are, where you are and where you want to go, let's talk about using the tarot as a tool for getting there. You really can use the tarot to manifest what you need and want on a physical level. This process begins with developing faith in yourself, believing that you have the power to make positive change in your life. Once you gain that faith, then you can start making small changes in your behaviour and outlook, in the way you do things and the pace you set yourself. Gradually, you'll start making bigger changes and taking bigger chances. As these pay off, you'll begin to accept only what is helpful and pleasing to you, because you sincerely believe that you deserve the very best.

Deciding What You Want

The first step in changing your physical reality is to allow yourself time to discover what it is you desire from your life, with the recognition that this may change from time to time. The problem most people face is that they simply don't know what it is they want. Work the exercises in the previous chapter until you are on fire with desire, and have a clear conviction of what you want.

Focusing on Your Goals

The next step in changing your physical reality is to change your mental outlook. Understand that you really can create a reality in which you are happy and fulfilled. You can find the perfect job, you can become powerful and effective, you can get what you need in all aspects of your life.

It's a matter of priority. You are not going to achieve everything right away or all at once. Work on one thing at a time. A change in career could help with stress and money woes. Working on your self-esteem will improve your chances of meeting potential friends and partners. Make a list of your priorities and tick them off as you accomplish them. Reward yourself as you accomplish your goals with the gift of a pretty tarot journal or tarot deck.

It's an excellent idea to draw a tarot card first thing in the morning to pinpoint and focus your actions during the day in terms of your current goal. You can ask the tarot what you have to do to achieve your purpose, whatever that may be.

- Pull a card from your deck and spend some time reading its meaning. Decide on your actions for the day.
- Set the card where you will see it, or carry it with you throughout the day to remind you to perform those actions.
- Keep a journal of what works and what doesn't, and note down your realizations of what the cards meant. You may see some evolution in the card meanings over time, but basic meanings will stay with you and help you mould your reality.

WHAT DO I NEED TO DO TODAY...

TO FIND THE JOB I WANT?

3 OF SWORDS This unhappy card tells me I need to face whatever it is that is making me unhappy. I can use that knowledge to find a better job. What I need to avoid is a job that has all the faults of the one I have now.

TO BRING HEALTHY COMMUNICATION INTO MY RELATIONSHIP?

8 OF COINS (reversed) A message of mastery in reverse, as this draw symbolizes, suggests that I need to let go of the idea that I can control this relationship, and stop trying to master my partner.

TO STAY ON COURSE WITH MY PLAN?

2 OF COINS The juggling card tells me that I need to pay attention to every aspect of the project, and ensure nothing is forgotten. I must think and act like a juggler to bring my plan to fruition.

Personal Manifestation

Do you sometimes feel powerless to make anything happen, or overpowered by the people and events around you? Work with the Magician card to help reclaim your personal power. Study the card. What are the tools on his table? Do you have some similar or corresponding tools in your trade that you would like to become better at using? What tools do you have in your personal tool chest? In what areas do you feel you need more power, better tools or more proficiency with those you have?

THE QUESTION: How can I become more powerful?

EXAMPLE READING

Jan feels ineffectual during disagreements with her partner, as well as in her career. She complains that the people around her seem to be constantly disempowering her.

IMMEDIATE IMPRESSIONS

The preponderance of Coins cards in the reading as a whole indicates the energies of money and tangible entities such as bodily health and possessions. | The areas where Jan is shown to need empowerment are mainly mental/intellectual, as highlighted by the two Swords cards. | The 5 of Coins points to a serious lack that must be faced and accepted. | The 'how to' cards are all Coins, which suggests Jan should face her problems squarely and be practical in her solutions.

WHERE DO I NEED MORE PERSONAL POWER?

PAGE OF SWORDS
This is the card of the secret agent. Jan has a tendency to consult others before acting. She needs to find the power to act independently and without approval.

HOW CAN I OBTAIN THIS POWER?

10 OF COINS
Jan ought to take strength from the permanent things in her life – those aspects that she can rely on, like her home and family. She needs to understand that she already has their permanent love and support.

CARD LAYOUT:

Keeping the Magician card above the layout, pull three cards to describe three areas where you need more personal power. Place them in a row, from left to right. Form a second row by drawing a further three cards to discover how to manifest power in these directions.

SUMMARY

Jan probably isn't headed for a pay rise in her current job, and this isn't her husband's fault. The love of her family is a great source of strength.

She can be more careful with her money and her possessions, remembering her husband isn't one of them. Her sense of disempowerment is partly due to her perception of not having enough money. Realizing this is the first step on her path to empowerment, perhaps also a different career. Keeping the cards representing how she can obtain the power she needs, along with the Magician, in a place she can see them will serve as a reminder of her realizations.

KNIGHT OF SWORDS

This card tells the querent to charge ahead. Again, Jan should feel empowered to act without being told what to do, or when and how to do it.

5 OF COINS

This 5 identifies a true lack and can indicate ill health or low finances. In this reading, it tells us that Jan needs to manifest power in regard to her low salary.

3 OF COINS (REVERSED)

Unfortunately for Jan, this is a big warning bell not to expect a pay rise or promotion. She can charge ahead with what she wants in life without waiting for these things to come to her.

4 OF COINS

Being the same suit as the card above, but a lower number, this card warns that Jan should slow down and reduce the speed at which she is accumulating. The message is frugality, which is of course the logical way to deal with a low salary.

Manifest Career Success

A tarot career consultation has many benefits. You may feel dissatisfied in your present job and wonder if there's something out there that would suit you better. You may deserve a pay increase. You may have lost your job and be looking for direction. Or, like the example given here, you may be carefully working toward your career goals but need advice on timing.

THE QUESTION: What is the best way to manifest my career goal?

CARD LAYOUT:

Mentally 'place' the question into the tarot deck. Shuffle and cut the cards as you prefer. Lay out the top five cards from the deck in a simple line spread, from left to right

EXAMPLE READING

Nathalie has worked as a teller in a bank for four years and would like to move into the mortgage department. She's looking for advice on whether to stay with her current company hoping for promotion, or to look elsewhere.

IMMEDIATE IMPRESSIONS

First, take note of obvious patterning. The appearance of two major arcana cards in a spread of five is important. It means that where Nathalie is now, and what will help her move forward, are significant life events (major arcana), as opposed to daily routines (the suits).

Three Wands cards is also significant. The Wands suit is associated with willpower, intuition and career. So these cards relate specifically to Nathalie's career.

WHERE AM I IN MY CAREER?

3 THE HIEROPHANT

This indicates that at the moment Nathalie is following the dictates of authority. While this offers some measure of safety and security, it doesn't allow for a great deal of personal growth. The Hierophant exists to serve the interests of society as a whole, not the individual.

WHAT HELPS ME MOVE UPWARD?

20 JUDGEMENT

Souls rise from the grave to the sound of angelic trumpets. To move upward in her career, Nathalie must answer the call of some higher purpose. Perhaps by working in mortgages she feels she can be of more help to people. The Judgement card is a sign to look for spiritual purpose in the mundane; to find something to lift your spirits or to help humanity.

SUMMARY

Cards 2 and 4 answer Nathalie's original question directly. Nathalie's best chance of manifesting her career goal is to seek a higher purpose and accept a heavy burden. A sense of higher purpose or helping others is often the only way to get through a huge burden of hard work, long hours and stress. By taking this advice, Nathalie should be able to pull herself out from under the boring thumb of the Hierophant and into more exciting areas where there is room to grow personally as well as financially.

 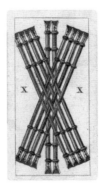 

WHAT HINDERS ME?

6 OF WANDS

The card in this position defines the problem Nathalie must recognize and deal with. She craves the outward trappings of success, but this need for victory and constant reassurance is hindering her. Nathalie needs to act more confidently and give praise to others, instead of needing it so much herself.

WHAT WILL GET ME TO WHERE I WANT TO GO?

10 OF WANDS

This is a card of heavy burden, usually borne for others, such as caring for a family member or a sick person. It seems to be pointing Nathalie towards the path of most resistance: either she has more work to do in her present job, or she should consider the extra workload of the new one. In short, she needs to work harder whether she stays or goes.

WHERE DO I WANT TO BE IN MY CAREER?

5 OF WANDS

The 5 card is midway between the Ace and the 10. This indicates that eventually Nathalie wants to become a middle manager. The meaning of the 5 of Wands is strife and conflict, which can be turned into cooperation.

Some people thrive on healthy debate. This card says that Nathalie wants to be in a position that challenges her.

Manifest Abundance

Possessing abundance is so much more than feeling satisfaction. It isn't merely having enough, it's having more than enough. Its presence is desirable in all aspects of our lives, not just our bank accounts. If we overflow with love and happiness, we have plenty of the same to share with others.

THE QUESTION: How can I manifest abundance in my life?

CARD LAYOUT:

Having decided on a specific area, begin the manifestation exercise by asking: 'How do I manifest abundance in X area of my life?' Shuffle and cut the deck of tarot cards as you prefer and lay out five cards left to right in a fan shape or arc.

EXAMPLE READING

I have a friend Helen who took in two families of stray cats: two mothers and 11 kittens. This was in addition to four cats of her own. She kept the two families in separate rooms and started contacting rescue organizations and putting up adoption flyers. When one of the mother cats died of feline leukaemia, the situation suddenly changed, because the kittens were no longer adoptable and rescue groups were no longer interested in helping. Helen's initial act of kindness has become a huge financial and emotional drain.

WHY IS THERE LACK IN THIS AREA OF MY LIFE?

21 THE WORLD

This lack has come into Helen's life simply because this is the way of the world. In Vedic literature it is stated over and over that the material world is simply a place of suffering. Lack is normal and part of being human. It takes special effort to manifest abundance in this world.

HOW CAN I REMEDY THIS LACK?

20 JUDGEMENT

In order to remedy this lack, Helen needs to discuss it with her higher power. Heed the call of Judgement Day, or experience a spiritual rebirth or re-dedication. The solution to the problem doesn't lie in earthly hands.

IMMEDIATE IMPRESSIONS

Three of the five cards are major arcana, indicating a major life event.

Note the appearance of the 8 of Coins. This card holds a positive or growing energy that radiates favourably in terms of Helen realizing abundance in this area of her life.

SUMMARY

The kittens have had a major effect on Helen's life and she has had a major effect on them.

Although the kittens' fate is for the most part out of her control, the overall outlook is nevertheless positive.

WHAT BRINGS ABUNDANCE INTO THIS AREA OF MY LIFE?

5 THE HIEROPHANT

The answer is to go with the recommendations of authority, in this case probably the veterinarians or, at least, people who have experience of feline leukaemia and strays. Helen should get their opinions and follow their instructions.

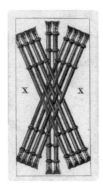

WHAT IS MY BEST CHOICE FOR NOW?

10 OF WANDS

Helen's best choice is to bear this burden of love as well as she is able. The energy of this card is that of parents who bear the burden of raising their children. Helen should do some research into treatments and therapies, continue the work already in progress and add to it, if possible.

WHAT IS THE NEW ABUNDANCE?

8 OF COINS

This 8 is a card of mastery, so it gives great hope that Helen will master the situation. If nothing else, she will gain abundant knowledge of the disease as well as all aspects of caring for stray cats.

Career Choices

The following list of 78 career choices forms the basis of yet another way the tarot can be used to help you think, decide and plan. It isn't meant as a surefire method to determine your next career move, but will get you out of your rut and start you thinking. The fact is that, no matter what the concern or situation, your tarot pack can be used to work it through. The people who say 'You can't do that with the tarot!' simply haven't applied their imagination.

Ask yourself the following questions and draw up to three cards to answer each. Look up your cards in the job description list to discover the tarot's message.

- What is my best job choice for now?
- Which career choices best suit my Body/Mind/Spirit?
- Which job will help me pay my bills?
- Which job will I find most satisfying?
- Which job opportunity is coming to me?

0 THE FOOL
venture capitalist, skydiver, rock climber

1 THE MAGICIAN
scientist, chemist, engineer

2 THE HIGH PRIESTESS
tarot reader, mystic or role related to divination, reiki therapist

3 THE EMPRESS
role in health or women's issues, gynaecologist, gardener

4 The Emperor

prime minister,
ultimate authority

5 The Hierophant

vicar or priest,
priestess

6 The Lovers

sex therapist,
dating agent

7 The Chariot

driver, leader
in the military

8 Justice

lawyer, judge,
court worker

9 The Hermit

writer, or an
actual hermit

10 The Wheel of Fortune

gambler, lottery worker

11 Strength

large animal
trainer, vet

12 The Hanged Man

volunteer or
charity worker

13 Death

worker in a funeral
director's or with
those suffering from
terminal illness

14 Temperance

gymnast, polarity
therapy

15 The Devil

bartender, worker
in media

16 THE TOWER
disaster relief
worker, explosives
technician

17 THE STAR life
coach, anything that
brings you joy

18 THE MOON
astronomer,
astronaut

19 THE SUN
childcare worker,
any outside work

20 JUDGEMENT
look to your higher
power for advice

21 THE WORLD
do it all, or
several things

2 OF WANDS freelancer

3 OF WANDS sailor, explorer, prospector

4 OF WANDS civil rights
worker, politician

5 OF WANDS mediator

6 OF WANDS courier for a
shipping company

7 OF WANDS Join a cause you believe in.

8 OF WANDS pilot, worker in the
aviation industry

9 OF WANDS Stay where you
are, stick with it.

10 OF WANDS care worker

PAGE OF WANDS religious counsellor,
church worker

KNIGHT OF WANDS Opt for
something completely different!

QUEEN OF WANDS Join a company
where you like the people.

KING OF WANDS Choose the job
that keeps you honest.

ACE OF WANDS role in male health

2 OF CUPS marriage counsellor

3 OF CUPS social or recreation director

4 OF CUPS substance abuse counsellor

5 OF CUPS teacher

6 OF CUPS photographic consultant

7 OF CUPS artist, actor, novelist

8 OF CUPS outdoor guide

9 OF CUPS wine taster, market researcher

10 OF CUPS Concentrate on your family and home life for now.

PAGE OF CUPS academic

KNIGHT OF CUPS office manager

QUEEN OF CUPS spouse, parent

KING OF CUPS doctor, nurse, therapist

ACE OF CUPS what you WANT to do

2 OF SWORDS court advocate

3 OF SWORDS relationship or grief counsellor

4 OF SWORDS worker at beach, mountain or any tourist resort

5 OF SWORDS insurance broker

6 OF SWORDS sailor, travel agent

7 OF SWORDS circus worker

8 OF SWORDS prison guard or worker

9 OF SWORDS therapist, psychiatrist

10 OF SWORDS suicide hotline worker

PAGE OF SWORDS intelligence agent

KNIGHT OF SWORDS military personnel

QUEEN OF SWORDS role in middle management

KING OF SWORDS role in senior management

ACE OF SWORDS ethics teacher or counsellor

2 OF COINS juggler, entertainer

3 OF COINS construction worker

4 OF COINS banker

5 OF COINS emergency services, hospital worker or role in medical supplies

6 OF COINS non-profit fundraiser

7 OF COINS farmer

8 OF COINS master craftsman

9 OF COINS investment or financial consultant

10 OF COINS estate agent or property investor

PAGE OF COINS special education worker

KNIGHT OF COINS role in utilities

QUEEN OF COINS pre-nuptial or marriage lawyer

KING OF COINS Get better at what you do now.

ACE OF COINS Start your own business.

The Power Pyramid: Job Choice

You may be considering several career or life choices and be uncertain about what's best for you and your future. This power pyramid helps you determine where your personal power lies and what choice is best for you. Before you lay out your pyramid, take some time to think about your options. It sounds obvious but the secret to career success is finding something you are good at and enjoy. Start on the right path, and advancement is that much easier.

THE QUESTION: What do I need to concentrate on?

CARD LAYOUT: Mentally place the question into the deck. Shuffle and cut the cards as you prefer. Lay out the top six cards from the deck in a pyramid shape with the first card on top.

EXAMPLE READING

Sarah was made redundant over a year ago. To make ends meet, she has taken on pet-sitting and cleaning jobs. She has also taken the opportunity to learn welding and is selling some of her metalwork art. The latter isn't bringing in much income so she feels guilty about devoting time to it.

IMMEDIATE IMPRESSIONS

Out of six cards, two are major arcana, indicating that this is a significant life decision, particularly since one is positioned at the pyramid's apex.

Three cards from the Coins suit suggest a decision involving earthly, physical, and/or financial considerations.

Five out of the six cards are reversed here. This highlights a large blockage of energy that Sarah needs to try and work through.

1

2   3

4   5   6

1 THE APEX: WHAT IS MY MOST IMPORTANT FOCUS?

0 THE FOOL The option that for Sarah feels most like jumping off a cliff without looking is to concentrate on her metalwork. The Fool tells us to take a chance and plunge headlong. Sarah has found herself a dream and she should pursue it.

2 FAMILY: THE LOVED ONES WHO SURROUND ME

4 THE EMPEROR (REVERSED) In reverse, the Emperor symbolizes an authority figure who is in some way blocked. Sarah needs to realize her independence apart from her family and friends and take full authority over her own life.

3 FINANCES: THE PRACTICAL MATTERS SURROUNDING ME

KNIGHT OF COINS (REVERSED) The other Knights are always getting into trouble, but this one is cautious. He considers every step before making a decision. As Coins is the suit of money, the home and everything tangible, Sarah needs to be particularly careful in these areas.

4 BODY: HOW TO FOCUS MY BODY ON THE APEX

9 OF COINS (REVERSED) The advice contained within the 9 of Coins is to make wise choices in the physical, as opposed to spiritual, realm. This may simply mean eating the right food, taking regular exercise, or making regular savings. Sarah's task is to find practical ways to make metalworking part of her life.

5 MIND: HOW TO FOCUS MY MIND ON THE APEX

6 OF COINS (REVERSED) Because it is upside down, the 6 of Coins indicates that Sarah is placed in a position of receiving charity, in this case lessons on metalworking. The balance may eventually turn itself around so that Sarah will be the one helping others, perhaps by sharing her new skills.

6 SPIRIT: HOW TO FOCUS MY SPIRIT ON THE APEX

4 OF WANDS (REVERSED) Appearing in reverse, this card indicates an alteration of energy in Sarah's spiritual realm. The inspiration she feels in artistic creation is a spiritual high. The message of the card is that, as she spends more time on her metalwork, she may find it becomes a form of prayer or divine communion.

SUMMARY

The true power of this pyramid layout is contained within the top card that directly answers the question. The other cards in the pyramid support this card by explaining how to make that choice happen. Reversed cards should be viewed as red flags that point out the hot spots or fires that need to be dealt with first. It is clear that Sarah has a lot of work to do in all aspects of her metalworking business. The seriousness of this is lessened by the fact it is a new venture and therefore the energies represented by the cards have yet to manifest themselves. That's another reason they all appear reversed.

The Power Pyramid: Investment

Another way to use the power pyramid is to help you make up your mind about a house purchase or any other large investment. Begin by making a list of all the things you need to consider. Then build yourself a pyramid, as I did here.

THE QUESTION: Is this the right house for me?

CARD LAYOUT:

Create a pyramid on paper by arranging the items of your list that relate to broad and external aspects on the bottom row, on up through the internal things, until you come to the peak, which will be the most important thing to you about your future house. The positional meaning signifies the present condition of the item and/or any warning you need to be aware of in its regard.

EXAMPLE READING

I carried out this reading when I was deciding whether to buy my house five years ago. Now I can look back and see how accurate it was!

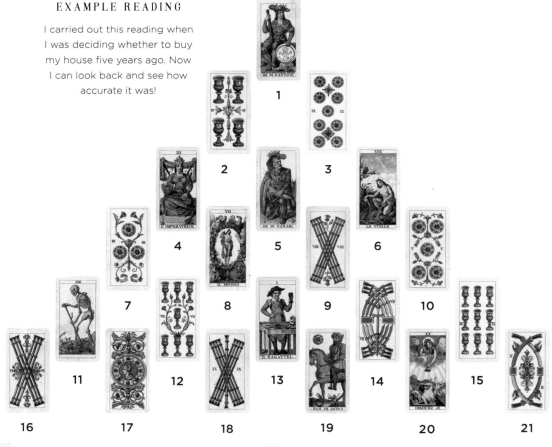

1 ASKING PRICE: KING OF WANDS This character has integrity. I am satisfied that the asking price was honest.

2 ROOF: 4 OF CUPS The roof's shingles had been positioned with a nail gun that was too powerful for the job. An example of excess in the wrong area.

3 SKYLIGHT: 9 OF COINS Number 9 on the luxury scale, my skylight has been a joy.

4 BATHROOMS: 3 THE EMPRESS Two large bathrooms could be considered bathrooms in abundance for just one person. It turned out there was an abundance of leaking water!

5 APPLIANCES: KING OF COINS The only appliances to come with the house were an oven and a dishwasher, so I have certainly had to be thrifty to buy the other appliances.

6 CEILING: 17 THE STAR The ceiling is fine. I'm still inspired to paint it like the night sky.

7 WINDOWS: 3 OF COINS Being double-glazed throughout, the windows do indeed save me some money on my electricity bill.

8 WALLS: 21 THE WORLD The walls are decorated in exactly the same way throughout.

9 FLOORS: 8 OF WANDS This 8 means that something is going to happen soon or quickly. Thanks to the leaks, the floors in the bathrooms rotted quickly.

10 DOORS: 5 OF COINS This card suggested a possible lack of security. After five years of broken doorknobs and rehanging doors, I see that its warning was less serious.

11 WATER: 13 DEATH The well failed the first water inspection and late last year my supply was completely cut off. This must have been the card's true meaning.

12 HEAT: 7 OF CUPS This positive card tallies with what has been a perfectly reliable heating system.

13 AIR CONDITIONING: 1 THE MAGICIAN The air conditioning works perfectly, using very little electricity.

14 ELECTRICITY: 7 OF SWORDS There have been no problems with the electricity so far, so I don't yet know what this warning refers to.

15 PHONE: 9 OF CUPS There is a little bit of noise on the line, as indicated by this card – but it's good enough!

16 NEIGHBOURS: 6 OF WANDS Good news in this area. I have two sets of very pleasant neighbours.

17 FOUNDATIONS: ACE OF COINS The Ace of Coins seems a very favourable sign for the foundations.

18 GROUNDS: 9 OF WANDS The two acres of lawn and woods have been a trial. This card encouraged me to persevere.

19 DRIVEWAY: KNIGHT OF COINS This card advised caution, but luckily a friend helped with the difficult job of laying the drainage pipe.

20 PLUMBING: 20 JUDGEMENT The Judgement card is so spiritual it's hard to relate it to the field of septic tanks. I simply took it as a positive sign.

21 ESTATE AGENT: 2 OF SWORDS I took this to mean that my estate agent was impartial.

Need/Want/Get: Lifestyle Choice

We all want so many things and, in many instances, we are entirely capable of obtaining them. But are they what we really need? The need/want/get tarot spread helps you appreciate the difference between needing and wanting. It encourages you to feel satisfied with what you eventually get. Having what you truly need is the real definition of abundance. Getting what you think you want may not be satisfying at all.

Be prepared for manifestation to take time. Even after you have attained your needs, it may be a while before you fully realize how your wants have also been satisfied. Be open to new definitions of success and abundance. Be open to 'getting it' in new cosmic ways.

THE QUESTION: What do I need/want/get?

CARD LAYOUT: Pull three cards from the deck to represent what you need/want/get, respectively.

EXAMPLE READING

Jason wants to use the tarot to give him guidance on how to give his bedroom a new look with a tranquil ambience. Create your own need/want/get spread on a daily basis to discover what you truly want and need in various aspects of your life.

NEED	WANT	GET

ACE OF WANDS (REVERSED)	7 OF COINS	8 JUSTICE

This card tells us that Jason needs to tone down the look of his bedroom. It's probably dark and full of wood and books. He needs to soften it to make it more peaceful.

What Jason wants to do is change a couple of small details and be done. But the way to accomplish what he truly needs is to make changes one at a time and give those changes time to work.

Signifying responsibility, this card suggests that Jason will get out of this what he puts in. A couple of small changes will lead to a small result. If he really wants to create a peaceful sleeping place, he will need to make bigger change.

MANIFESTING WHAT YOU NEED

After working the need/want/get spread in a particular area of your life, work toward some sort of consensus or agreement between your needs and wants. When you have this resolved and can accept how your need fulfils your want, the next step is to ask the tarot how to get what you need. Use the card that describes the need as a starting point or significator. Place it at the top of your workspace.

Shuffle the rest of the deck and draw a card to answer each of the following questions:

CARD 1 What can I do today to manifest what I need?

CARD 2 Where can I get what I need?

CARD 3 How can I have faith while my needs manifest?

CARD 4 How can I acquire what I need?

CARD 5 How can I keep it once I get it?

Work the answers that the cards give you; this is the process to undertake to manifest your needs. Don't be surprised if the 7 of Coins (patience) or the Star (you already have everything you need) make an appearance.

THE QUESTION: What do I need/want/get in my relationship?

You can work this 12-card variation to understand the state of your relationship.

CARD 1 What you need

CARD 2 What the other person needs

CARD 3 What the relationship needs

CARD 4 What you want

CARD 5 What the other person wants

CARD 6 What the relationship wants

CARD 7 What you 'really' want

CARD 8 What the other person 'really' wants

CARD 9 What the relationship 'really' wants

CARD 10 What you get

CARD 11 What the other person gets

CARD 12 What the relationship gets

Open Yourself to Love

This is a good spread to perform should you find yourself lonely on 14th February!

THE QUESTION: **How can I manifest love in my life?**

CARD LAYOUT: Mentally 'place' the question into your tarot deck. Then shuffle and cut the deck as you prefer. Lay out the cards in the shape of a heart, starting 5 from the bottom and working up one side, then the other, and finally laying down the central card. The two arms of the heart represent two paths you can take to get to a place of receptivity to love. Work both paths simultaneously or choose one.

EXAMPLE READING

In manifesting our desires, we need to find a balance between specific and open-ended questions. We use terms like Mr Right, soulmate, perfect partner, when love and fulfilment are what we truly want. In this example reading, Vicky, who doesn't have much experience in love and relationships, would like to know how she can open herself to love.

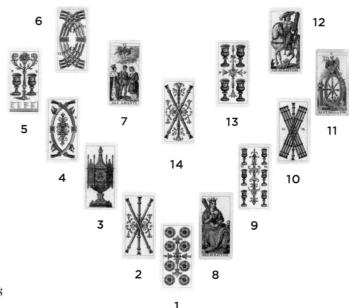

IMMEDIATE IMPRESSIONS

The energy of movement and change in this spread is emphasized by the appearance of a number 6 in the positional number 6.

The Ace and 2 of Cups (new relationship and love) along with the Lovers card all appear on the left curve of the heart, so following the natural flow through these stages seems a better, more obvious choice for Vicky.

SUMMARY

The 14 cards Vicky has drawn are merely the beginning of her work in this area of her life. She is beginning with a set of skills (mastery: 8 of Coins) and she needs to use these on her step-by-step journey to love. The dominion represented by her final card is a birthright that she will claim when she becomes a mature lover.

1 MYSELF NOW: 8 OF COINS It's uncanny how often this card makes an appearance in a relationship spread. It's a card of mastery, usually in the context of excelling in your profession. When love or a relationship is in question, it points to control issues. Love means caring cooperation, give and take. Vicky needs to address her desire to be master of a relationship, or to be mastered.

2 STAGE 1 ON THE PATH TO LOVE: 3 OF WANDS The first stage that Vicky will need to pass through on the way to becoming receptive to love is exploration. She should get out there.

3 STAGE 2: ACE OF CUPS Once Vicky has begun exploring, she will very quickly meet new people and make new friends.

4 STAGE 3: 2 OF SWORDS At stage three on her path to love, Vicky will be faced with a tough decision. She may have to choose between two likely candidates.

5 STAGE 4: 2 OF CUPS This draw suggests that Vicky will make the right choice and enter into a serious long-term relationship.

6 STAGE 5: 6 OF SWORDS After entering this relationship, Vicky will either travel or move. She needs to be prepared for this.

7 STAGE 6: THE LOVERS You face a choice with this card. Do you want love or lust?

8 ABILITY TO LISTEN TO MYSELF: QUEEN OF WANDS The friend card tells Vicky that she should trust and listen to herself as she would a best friend. If she is her own best friend, others will seek her friendship also.

9 ABILITY TO NURTURE MYSELF: 6 OF CUPS Symbolizing childhood nostalgia, this draw tells Vicky to go back in time and nurture her inner child.

10 TRULY LOVING MYSELF: 9 OF WANDS Vicky is going to need perseverance on her quest. Finding love and opening yourself up to its possibility takes practice.

11 LISTENING WITH PATIENCE AND UNDERSTANDING: 10 THE WHEEL OF FORTUNE Vicky can create love and luck in her life by learning to listen.

12 ABILITY TO COOPERATE: KNIGHT OF WANDS Like the Knight, Vicky needs to know when enough is enough and so make a daring departure.

13 ABILITY TO COMMUNICATE: 4 OF CUPS The card of excess tells Vicky that, if or when a relationship becomes too much for her, she needs to talk the problem through with her partner and stand up for herself.

14 LOVE MADE MANIFEST: 2 OF WANDS By following either or both of the heart paths, Vicky will attain dominion over her ablity to love.

Manifest the King/Queen of My Heart

This spread can help you break a cycle of choosing inappropriate partners, and open the door to the kind of romantic relationship that nurtures and fulfils. It can also strengthen an existing relationship. Perform it in the evening for best results.

CARD LAYOUT: First pull out the King, Queen and 2 of Cups from your deck. Find yourself two matching champagne flutes or very nice wineglasses, and a larger bowl or cup. Put a pair of green (representing the heart chakra) candles in matching fire-safe holders. Place the 2 of Cups card in the centre of your table or altar and the larger bowl or cup just behind it, empty. To one side of this place the King of Cups and to the other the Queen of Cups. Behind both cards there should be a glass full of water and a green candle.

Manifestation

Create sacred space for protection. Light the two candles and request the help of your higher power. Recite the following aloud (you can substitute Queen for King etc. if this is more applicable):

Goddess bring my love to me
Bring me the King of my heart
Bring to me the mate that is right for me
Him, the one that's meant for me

Goddess bring my love to him
Bring the Queen of his heart to him
Bring to him the mate that is right for him
Me, the one that's meant for him

Goddess bring us together
Bring these true mates together
Let us recognize each other
For the highest good in truth and love
Goddess bring us together.

Pour a little water from each glass into the empty cup in the middle and move them a little closer to the central cup. In doing so, you are drawing the King and Queen together.

Let the candles burn a while until you feel peace and energy flow, then extinguish them so that you can burn them again the following evening.

Note down your thoughts, feelings and impressions. Did you get a clear picture of a person or a sense of their personality?

Perform this manifestation ritual nightly from the new to full moon to increase attraction, or from full to full moon to first remove obstacles and then increase attraction. It's more effective if you perform it repeatedly rather than letting the candles burn out all at once. Plan ahead so that you don't miss a night and weaken the effect.

Heartmate Manifestation

When your desire has reached such intensity that you want to declare it to the universe, use this manifestation to get your Heartmate moving in your direction.

MENTAL PREPARATION

Keep the knowledge you gain from answering these questions in mind as you perform the manifestation.

CARD 1 What do I need to do to bring my Heartmate to me?

CARD 2 Tell me of my Heartmate so that I will recognize them.

CARD 3 What do I need to understand about my Heartmate?

CARD 4 What does my Heartmate need most from me?

CARD 5 What prevents my Heartmate from coming to me?

CARD 6 What can I do to make myself ready to meet my Heartmate?

MANIFESTATION

To perform the manifestation, you will need a card that depicts the qualities you most desire in a mate. It may be one of the cards you picked during your mental preparation, or a different one. Have ready your chosen card, a red candle and some scented oil.

- Prop the card up on a clear workspace or altar so that you can see it comfortably while you prepare the candle.
- Breathing deeply, chant softly:

  My soulmate, my lifemate, my heartmate, my lovemate, my sexmate,
  Come to me, come to me, come to me.
- Use the tip of one index finger to rub the scented oil lightly all over the candle.
- Set the candle in its fire-safe holder and light it.
- Continue chanting as you gaze at the flame and perceive its heat sending your heartfelt desire upward to the heavens where dreams come true and perfect happiness exists.
- Let the candle burn to completion. Note your thoughts, feelings and impressions. Do you get a sense of when or how your mate will manifest? Don't be surprised if you meet a new friend or hear from an old one soon afterwards.

THE QUESTION: Who is your ideal mate?

CARD LAYOUT: Choose one card that represents your most desired mate. You will also need a red candle and some scented oil.

KING OF CUPS

Also known as the King of Love.

QUEEN OF CUPS

Perfect wife and mother. The Queen of my heart.

KING OF WANDS

Fiery, passionate, open and honest.

QUEEN OF WANDS

Worthy of worship. A true friend.

ACE OF WANDS

A very sexy lover.

KING OF COINS

Dependable provider.

8 OF COINS

Master of his trade.

THE WORLD

She has the World at her fingertips. She's on top of the World.

THE LOVERS

A lover sent by an angel.

KNIGHT OF SWORDS

Dashing swashbuckler.

When Enough is Enough

When the Death card shows up in a relationship spread, it doesn't mean that someone is about to die, rather that the relationship is heading for an end. Only the very strongest, deepest and longest-lasting relationships can weather the bad times and survive periods of doubt. Use this nine-card relationship spread if you are feeling unsure of a relationship, romantic or otherwise, one-on-one or within a group or team.

LETTING GO

When you read the cards that appear in this layout, you may find that your expectations of your relationship are unrealistic and that the differences between you and your partner are irreconcilable. It's very hard to decide to end a relationship. We want to reclaim the joy, wonder and affection we had when it was new. It can be hard to find someone we feel compatible with, whom we can communicate and get along with, let alone someone who fills us with passion and life. Beginning again can take enormous strength, but accept it as an ongoing organic process. Nothing is lost. Experience and self-knowledge are always gained and carried with us into the future.

On the other hand, this spread can help you re-evaluate and change your expectations of the relationship, so that you see it more realistically, and become more self-sufficient in creating your own happiness and less dependent on your partner to create it for you.

THE BIG PICTURE

Working larger spreads like this one of nine cards takes a lot of time and energy. It can be tempting to look only at the outcome or advice card and simply go with it. That shortchanges the value of the tarot and what it can do for you. The outcome and advice of the tarot are more effectively understood in context. It's good practice to deal out the cards face down and only turn them over one by one, taking plenty of time to consider each card individually. Then go back and study the recurrence of suit, number and symbols, even colours. Look for patterns created by the whole picture of the layout, such as ascending numbers, to glean more information about both yourself and your question.

You may want to draw another spread to explore further the options regarding what can help with the relationship.

THE QUESTION: **Is this relationship over?**

CARD LAYOUT: Deal out a grid of nine cards in three rows.

**YOUR EXPECTATIONS
OF YOUR PARTNER**

**YOUR EXPECTATIONS
OF THE RELATIONSHIP**
What you want to get out of it.

WHY YOU ARE DISAPPOINTED
Where have things
gone wrong?

**YOUR PARTNER'S
EXPECTATIONS
OF YOU**

**YOUR PARTNER'S EXPECTATIONS
OF THE RELATIONSHIP**
What they wanted to get out of it.

**WHY YOUR PARTNER
IS DISAPPOINTED** Where
things have gone wrong.

PROBABLE OUTCOME Where the
relationship is heading if things
continue as they are.

**WHO OR WHAT CAN HELP
THE RELATIONSHIP?**

**PROBABLE OUTCOME IF
THIS HELP IS TAKEN**

chapter five

Access the Power of Your Mind

Several systems of classification are used to describe the mind and intelligence and their different states, such as consciousness, unconsciousness, subconsciousness and dream state. In the ancient texts of Vedic India the mind is part of the subtle body that is the first covering of the jivatma or spirit soul. The soul is composed of eternity, knowledge and bliss. In the material world, the soul takes on both a subtle body and a gross body. The subtle body is composed of mind, intelligence and ego, and goes by many names, such as astral body, aura or auric field. The gross body is composed of blood, guts, bones and so on. The soul travels this material world born in one body, dying only to be born again in a new body, according to the vastly intricate laws of karma – now as a human, then as an animal, and sometimes as a plant or microbe. It is the gross body that changes. The subtle body stays with the soul taking on impressions and information life after life.

Transcending the Physical State

In the normal state of consciousness the deep long-term memory of the subtle body is inaccessible to the gross physical brain. Of course, sometimes there is bleed-through, in geniuses like Mozart, for example, and others who display a lifetime of knowledge and skill while still small children. In an altered state of consciousness, these past-life memories as well as spiritual Truths, with a capital T, can be accessed. Some people alter their consciousness with chemicals and do indeed perceive beyond the veil of physical reality. But gross chemical alteration can only take you so far with the subtle body. The altered perception lasts only until the liver and kidneys flush out the chemicals. How spiritual is that? In this day and age, the recommended way to access your eternal spiritual reality is to chant or sing holy names. Thus so many religions have a tradition and practice of chanting prayers and singing songs of holy names. This is the basis of all sorts of meditation. Focusing the mind and ears on transcendental sounds allows the conscious mind to transcend its gross material boundaries and access spiritual reality.

The Power of the Tarot

With the tarot, we focus the mind on the pictures and symbols. By their nature as archetypes, the cards act as portholes or keys to unlock the doors of perception. In this chapter and the next we make more subtle use of the tarot than in earlier chapters, beginning with an examination of the power of the mind.

The big secret of tarot is that it can be used for so much more than mere fortune telling. It is a magical self-help tool of great power. We are accustomed to using such a tiny portion of the brain, and there's really no measure of the power of the mind. Let's start out with the premise that the power of the mind is unlimited and that by using it you can achieve anything and everything you set your mind to. That's a daunting concept. If you could have anything you wanted, what would it be? Why not set your mind to it?

Revealing the Inner Self

We all get caught up in identifying ourselves with the job we do, the people we know, the place we live, the colours we like, the recognition we've earned and all those temporary, external things by which our lives can be marked, graded and recognized by our peers. Yet, internally, we may be very far removed from all that. We change and grow. Use the tarot to become more aware of your own inner life.

When you open your mind to the universe of possibility, everything you come in contact with becomes a priceless gem of wisdom, a lesson to be learned, a truth to be understood, a gift of God. You can use the tarot to help recognize and understand today's gift. Calm and clear your mind. Open it to receptivity. Prepare to receive a gift.

Ask one of the following questions while you shuffle the cards:

- What is my lesson today?
- What is the gift I need to take possession of?
- What is the wisdom I am offered?
- Who is my teacher today?
- Why am I stuck in this situation?
- How did I get here?

THE QUESTION: What is my lesson today?

CARD LAYOUT: Pull one card and think about its meaning in the context of the question you asked.

EXAMPLE READING

Learn the lesson of the card. Here are 22 lessons I've learned from the major arcana, to get you started.

4 THE EMPEROR
teaches me the value of my masculine side.

5 THE HIEROPHANT
teaches me my reliance on external conscience.

10 THE WHEEL OF FORTUNE
teaches me always to try.

11 STRENGTH
teaches me that I am strong in many ways.

16 THE TOWER
teaches me to hold on to hope.

17 THE STAR
teaches me to believe in myself.

0 THE FOOL

teaches me how to start again from square one.

1 THE MAGICIAN

teaches me the worth and use of tools.

2 THE HIGH PRIESTESS

teaches me the beauty of mystery.

3 THE EMPRESS

teaches the value of my feminine, nurturing side.

6 THE LOVERS

teaches me that I always have a choice.

7 THE CHARIOT

teaches me self-discipline.

8 JUSTICE

teaches me the difference between good and evil.

9 THE HERMIT

teaches me the power of solitude.

12 THE HANGED MAN

teaches me the joy of burdens and hardship.

13 DEATH

teaches me that nothing material lasts.

14 TEMPERANCE

teaches me the importance of balance.

15 THE DEVIL

teaches me that I am only human.

18 THE MOON

teaches me that my darkness is also me.

19 THE SUN

teaches me to see the simple, naked truth.

20 JUDGEMENT

teaches me there is always a second chance.

21 THE WORLD

teaches me to strive for completeness.

Chakras

Gaining an appreciation of the seven chakras, or energy centres of the body, is a great way to learn more about yourself and to understand what is going on in your life.

To give you a brief overview, here is the shorthand system I use:

7TH OR CROWN CHAKRA

white – the crown of the head; connection with the divine and infinite, spiritual tasks, life purpose issues.

6TH OR THIRD EYE-CHAKRA

purple – eyes, head, brain, mind; intuition, intellect, imagination.

5TH OR THROAT CHAKRA

blue – throat, mouth, voice; speech, communication, creative expression.

4TH OR HEART CHAKRA

green/pink – heart, lungs; feelings, loving relationships.

3RD OR SOLAR-PLEXUS CHAKRA

yellow – stomach, digestion; will, identity, self-esteem.

2ND OR SACRAL CHAKRA

orange – reproductive organs, lower back; sexuality, creativity.

1ST OR ROOT CHAKRA

red/black – excretive organs, feet, bones; basis of your existence, physical and financial survival, your life's seat or situation.

CARD LAYOUT:

Deal 14 cards in seven pairs, one for each of the seven chakras, working from the base chakra up (deal the 1st chakra first).

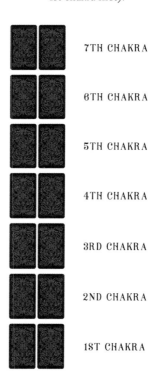

7TH CHAKRA

6TH CHAKRA

5TH CHAKRA

4TH CHAKRA

3RD CHAKRA

2ND CHAKRA

1ST CHAKRA

THE QUESTION: **What can I do to improve my life as a whole?**

EXAMPLE READING

Richard suffers from back pain and has recently lost his job. Refer to the card layout opposite for how to lay the cards out.

THE STATE OF YOUR CHAKRA

THE TAROT'S ADVICE

1ST CHAKRA

4 OF WANDS (REVERSED)

This upside-down 4 means it's not yet time to celebrate freedom! Intellectually, Richard feels free to pursue his desires, but maybe physically, deep down, he is scared and worried, hence the reversal.

3 OF COINS (REVERSED)

The advice seems to be not to carry on with the same work, but to seek a different path. Richard needs to turn his ideas of work, labour and money upside down.

KING OF CUPS

The King is wonderful reassurance that Richard is a loving and understanding man.

2ND CHAKRA

7 OF COINS

He has all the raw material for a healthy, loving relationship, so he need only be patient, as this card advises.

IMMEDIATE IMPRESSIONS

The majority of cards (see also pages 150–51) are minor arcana, signifying that the energy present in Richard's chakras is normal, not life changing.

Including the Emperor (in the 4th chakra position) there are four cards of the number 4, indicating balanced energy. Eight of the fourteen cards are reversed. It makes sense that pain would come from blocked energy.

Both of the 3rd chakra cards are reversed, as are the 1st chakra cards – so it would seem the lower back pain is caused by blockages in the solar plexus and root chakras, rather than the sacral chakra itself.

3RD CHAKRA

KING OF SWORDS (REVERSED)

This card indicates that Richard is struggling with an intellectual or ethical issue in the realm of willpower and self-identity.

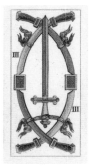

21 THE WORLD (REVERSED)

He needs to step back from the idea of finding a final solution. Complete integration is delayed or lessened right now, although it is certainly possible in the future if he can turn things around.

4TH CHAKRA

4 THE EMPEROR

Richard is the Emperor of his own heart. He isn't in a romantic relationship but wishes he were. He is also somewhat estranged from both siblings and parents. The hard, authoritative figure of the Emperor may shed some light on why this is.

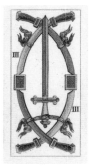

3 OF SWORDS (REVERSED)

This card tells Richard to let go of sorrow and not be so sensitive to the pain in his heart and emotions. (To banish the 3 of Swords, see page 154.)

5TH CHAKRA

4 OF COINS (REVERSED)

The throat chakra has some energy of greed or possessiveness about it. A reversed card in this position can mean that communications are coming out garbled or that creative expression is stymied.

7 THE CHARIOT

The Chariot preaches self-control. In the throat chakra position, think before you speak is a practical interpretation.

THE STATE OF YOUR CHAKRA

THE TAROT'S ADVICE

6TH CHAKRA

5 THE HIEROPHANT
(REVERSED)

Mentally there is some
blockage or problem in
the way Richard thinks
society perceives him.
He may feel that losing his
job was society's way of
telling him something.

4 OF SWORDS

The advice is to take a break.
A period of rejuvenation will
give Richard a new mental
outlook, and probably help
his back stop hurting.

7TH CHAKRA

8 OF COINS

Mastery of a skill or situation,
symbolized by this 8, is the
energy present in Richard's
crown chakra.

KNIGHT OF COINS
(REVERSED)

The advice card seems
to discourage caution
and encourage hastiness.
Perhaps Richard is being
over-cautious in his spiritual
life and needs to develop
more confidence in his
understanding of his
spiritual path.

SUMMARY

The preponderance of Coins and Swords is not surprising. Richard is
faced with money issues and is relying on his intellect to deal with them.
However, he is in a good place overall, as shown by the four number
4s and the positive cards in his heart chakra. His lower back pain may
be the result of strain in another area. He should get this checked out
by a professional.

Affirmation

You need a positive mental attitude to excel in the art and science of living. Focusing on your negative problems only gives strength to their power over your life.

Positive affirmations can be as simple as 'Today I will have a good day' or as complex as a detailed business plan.

There are many decks out there with this principle in mind. Sally Hill has added 78 affirmations to the Rider-Waite deck, called *Tarot Affirmations*. I've used the Zerner-Farber *Gifts of the Goddess* affirmation deck to answer a daily 'What affirmation do I need today?' and found it very powerful in terms of assimilating life's lessons and improving my mental attitude. Some other non-tarot affirmation decks are: Louise L. Hay's *I Can Do It Cards* and *Power Thought Cards*; Wayne W. Dyer's *Inner Peace Cards* and Sonia Cafe's *Angel Meditation Cards*. They are all wonderful for breaking bad habits, for strengthening and improving the mind and for creating lasting change.

AFFIRMATION EXERCISES

Taking one suit at a time, write affirmations for each card (the court cards already have affirmations included in their definitions – see pages 84–99.)

Rewrite the list of major arcana affirmations to better suit your life, your path and your worldview.

Be specific in your question to the cards and ask 'What affirmation do I need today to...

- help with my work?
- help me make wise choices?
- help me heal?
- help me cope?'

THE QUESTION: What affirmation do I need today?

CARD LAYOUT: Using only the major arcana cards, perform a one-card draw every day for a month, asking one of the questions below left. Place the card you draw where you will be sure to see it throughout the day.

4 THE EMPEROR
I am the absolute best authority in my life.

5 THE HIEROPHANT
I learn from other cultures and traditions.

10 THE WHEEL OF FORTUNE
Good or bad, luck is a gift for growth.

11 STRENGTH
I am strong enough to compromise.

16 THE TOWER
I will weather surprises with good humour.

17 THE STAR
I am a particle of the Goddess. I love the Goddess and thank Her for Her love.

0 THE FOOL

I am not afraid
to start anew.

1 THE MAGICIAN

I have the
ability to manifest
my desire.

2 THE HIGH PRIESTESS

I see beyond the veil to
what is most important
and useful to know.

3 THE EMPRESS

Today I will
nurture myself.

6 THE LOVERS

Every aspect
of my being is
replete with love.

7 THE CHARIOT

I am strong in
self-control.

8 JUSTICE

I do not have to
tolerate anyone's
bad behaviour.

9 THE HERMIT

I am wise.

**12 THE HANGED
MAN**

Today's sacrifice is
tomorrow's reward.

13 DEATH

I allow myself to
complete a stage
and close it.

14 TEMPERANCE

When I feel unbalanced,
I will allow myself
to pause to restore
my equilibrium.

15 THE DEVIL

I can look the
other way and
resist temptation.

18 THE MOON

I am in tune
with the Earth
and the Moon.

19 THE SUN

Sunlight charges the air
with love. With every
breath, I breathe in love.

20 JUDGEMENT

Today I will
try my best.

21 THE WORLD

From my crown to
my feet, I am whole
and complete.

Affirming the Swords Suit

Another way of using the tarot cards for mental affirmation is to decide what you want and gaze at the card while mentally affirming its qualities and energy. The following four examples use cards from the Swords suit.

AFFIRM THE END OF HEARTACHE: Banish the 3 of Swords

CARD LAYOUT: Pull the 3 of Swords card from your deck and fasten it to whatever you are wearing so that the picture faces your heart.

Face your heartache, its causes and how you came to be in such pain. Allow the card to symbolize all of that for you.

- Carry the card with you for several hours while you work through your heartache, until you feel ready to let go of it completely.

- When you do feel ready, prepare a small fire in a metal cauldron, in your fireplace or outside in a sensible place.

- Burn any items that you associate with your heartache. Watch them disappear and turn to ash.

- Pull the 3 of Swords from your heart and place it in the flames, affirming aloud:

  I am done with heartache, sorrow and emotional pain.
  I release it and let it go.
  I don't need it any more.
  I am done with it.
  Heartache is gone.

- Feel your heartache lift and disappear. Cherish the new lighter feeling in your heart. Don't dwell any longer on the heartache you have just released.

- Alternatively, if you don't want to destroy your card, waft it through the smoke until you feel it is fully cleansed of all the negative emotions you placed into it.

AFFIRM REVITALIZATION: Manifest the 4 of Swords

CARD LAYOUT: Place the 4 of swords somewhere you can see it easily, and refer to it
to keep focused on your purpose.

Identify and meditate on what is draining your energy, or how you
have become tired and in need of revitalization. This is what will
be purged with each exhalation.

- Now picture yourself and your life, full of energy and health. Picture all the positive things you want to accomplish. (Alternatively, work with one area, one chakra or one issue.) Take up a rainbow candle (with six colours, or six colours plus white, or just the one colour that symbolizes the area you want to work on).

- Holding the candle, breathe on it, and rub it with fragrant oil. Mentally place the picture of that whole, healthy revitalized you into the candle.

- Light the candle and secure it safely. Gaze at its flame.

- Draw that positive mental image along with all healing energy into your lungs deeply and freely. Draw in life, love and happiness. Experience wholeness.

- With each exhalation, purge yourself – your mind, your heart, your psyche, your spirit, your body – of the lethargy, the negativity, the hurt, the pain, the disease and the causes.

  In
  Out

- As you continue this calming breathing exercise, entranced by the flame and your own precious breath, feel the negativity leave and positivity take its place, until finally you are breathing out positive energy as well as in.

  In
  Out

- Keep the card visible to remind you of the calm positive state you achieved.

CARD LAYOUT: Pull the 7 of Swords card from your deck and place it somewhere clearly visible. You will need a black candle for this spell. Black is a great colour for absorbing negativity and for grounding.

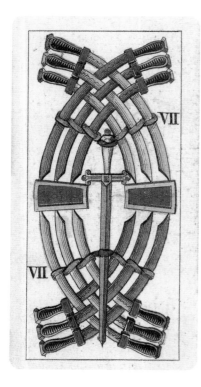

The 7 of Swords is a somewhat negative card by its nature, so be very careful and strong in your intent before invoking its energies. What was stolen may be a material object or your heart, or the energy specific to a chakra.

It's absolutely vital you are certain of the person who stole from you because you will be dealing with that person's energy.

- Light the candle.
- Gaze into the candle's flame and breathe deeply till you feel calm and relaxed.
- Study the 7 of Swords.
- Visualize the thief who stole from you.
- Visualize the thing stolen from you.
- Clap the thief in irons.
- Take back what is rightfully yours. Feel it in your hands. Embrace it, name it, make it yours.
- Chant the following:

    It's mine, I want it back.
    It's mine, I have it back.
    I am whole.

- Repeat until you believe it.
- Turn the card over. The spell is done.
- Let the candle burn down till it is gone.

AFFIRM THE END OF ANXIETY: Banish the 9 of Swords

CARD LAYOUT: Take the 9 of Swords card from your deck. For this spell, you will also need a beautiful flower or some other symbol of freedom from anxiety. It can be anything happy and carefree, like a bright yellow candle.

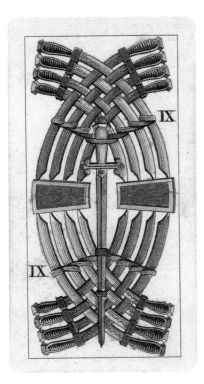

Gaze at the 9 of Swords and acknowledge the stress and anxiety you feel.

- Repeat one of these statements or craft your own.

  Stress and anxiety disturb my sleep.
  I am not dealing with worry very well right now.
  I am overwhelmed by my problems.

- Once you have 'owned' your stress and anxiety, place the card flat on the table and put your worry-free symbol on top of it. It will overshadow and overcome your worry.

- Now repeat one or more of the following, or craft your own statement:

  I can sleep soundly.
  I can stop worrying.
  My problems will still be there when I am ready to deal with them.
  I will worry to the appropriate degree, and then I will relax.

- Feel the tension leave your shoulders. Allow yourself to relax.

- Keep your positive affirmation in your mind all day.

Healing

Serious illness can be overwhelming. Understanding your illness, its causes and the treatments can turn into a second full-time job. You may see several doctors and a whole gamut of healthcare workers, such as nurses, physical therapists, nutritionists and so on. The tarot can be used as a tool to put it all together and help you understand your disease and what to do about it, as is shown by the real-life example I share with you here.

Your illness or life concern will be specific to you. You can choose card position definitions to describe it and better understand your situation.

KNIGHT OF
WANDS
Today

1 THE
MAGICIAN
What supports
me?

KING OF SWORDS
Obstacles
to healing.

6 OF COINS
(REVERSED)

Current diagnosis

17 THE STAR
(REVERSED)
Current
prognosis.

16 THE TOWER
Current
treatment

THE QUESTION: What is the best way to deal with this situation?

CARD LAYOUT: Shuffle the deck while thinking of your own highest good and opening your mind to the wisdom of the universe. You can lay the cards out in any way that makes the most sense to you. This layout is interpreted on pages 160–63.

0 THE FOOL
You.

EXAMPLE READING

Beverly is 65 years old and has had four bouts of cancer, three of which were treated with surgery. Her colon cancer, treated with chemotherapy, is currently in remission but she often feels weak and tired. She is also diabetic and suffers from arthritis.

3 THE EMPRESS
Tomorrow

ACE OF COINS
Aids to healing

5 OF COINS
(REVERSED)
Let this go.

14 TEMPERENCE
(REVERSED)
Honour this.

15 THE DEVIL
Improving
current
prognosis.

2 OF SWORDS
Improving
current
treatment.

KING OF COINS
Improving
communication.

ACE OF SWORDS
Your disease.

19 THE SUN
(REVERSED)
Its cause.

9 OF CUPS
(REVERSED)
Its cure.

1. YOU

0 THE FOOL

Beverly is at the beginning of a new stage of life. The Fool may refer to her recent interest in metaphysical approaches to healing, such as using the tarot, chakras and positive affirmations, and treatments like aromatherapy, acupuncture, reiki, etc.

2. YOUR DISEASE

ACE OF SWORDS

Swords can indicate scalpels and thus a chance of surgery, or needles. They can also refer to psychic surgery that is done energetically with a crystal point and intense intent. This card prompted me to ask Beverly what new idea her healthcare providers had come up with lately, referring back to the Fool. A few days later she found out that she had new damage to her lower back.

3. ITS CAUSE

19 THE SUN (REVERSED)

We dealt the cards thinking of Beverly's cancer. It's hard to think of the sun as the cause of illness, although this may explain why the card is reversed. There's no doubt sunburn can have fatally serious consequences. One other known cause of cancer is naturally occurring radiation This may lie at the root of Beverly's disease.

Another way to interpret this card is that, like sunrise, the nature of Beverly's illnesses are the natural way of the world.

4. ITS CURE

9 OF CUPS (REVERSED)

The 9 of Cups is the wish card, so its appearance in the 'cure' position is a very good sign that Beverly's cancer will be cured or at least in remission for a long time. But the fact that the card is reversed means there is work to be done, or that the cure is delayed. Beverly needs to adjust her perspective and learn to be satisfied on a different level.

5. WHAT DO I NEED TO KNOW ABOUT MY CURRENT DIAGNOSIS?

6 OF COINS (REVERSED)

When this card appears reversed it should be read as a sign to stop being so generous and to put yourself first. This isn't selfishness; it's what you need to do sometimes so that you can share again from a place of fullness and abundance. Beverly gets confused about her exact diagnosis and prognosis and, as we see here, both cards are reversed. I suspect that she may be giving her doctors the benefit of the doubt and that she needs to be more assertive about asking them to explain her situation in language that she can understand.

6. WHAT DO I NEED TO KNOW ABOUT MY CURRENT PROGNOSIS?
17 THE STAR (REVERSED)

The Star is a card of inspiration. It tells you that you have everything you need within you. Its appearance in reverse means that you have not tapped into that full potential. Beverly may have more options than she is aware of. The card points to inner wisdom and trust in oneself.

7. WHAT DO I NEED TO KNOW ABOUT MY CURRENT TREATMENT?

16 THE TOWER

The Tower predicts a major change is coming in Beverly's treatment sooner rather than later. The good thing for Beverly is that the Tower always leads you where you wanted to go anyway, but were not going on your own.

8. HOW CAN I IMPROVE ON MY CURRENT PROGNOSIS?
15 THE DEVIL

The Devil card exposes ignorance and trickery or self-deception. Beverly is in denial about something. There is no chance of improving her health outlook if she does not admit how bad it is or what needs to be done.

9.HOW CAN I IMPROVE ON MY CURRENT TREATMENT?

2 OF SWORDS

The 2 of Swords in this position indicates that there is no moving forward here. I suspect that Beverly needs to follow the treatments she has already been given more strictly, especially the diet and exercise regime for her diabetes and arthritis.

10. HOW CAN I IMPROVE COMMUNICATION WITH MY HEALTHCARE PROVIDERS?

KING OF COINS

The message of this card is that Beverly can improve communications with her providers by complimenting them and telling them how good they are. They are skilled at what they do and some small recognition of that will help them open up and see her as a person, and therefore take a more personal interest in her case.

11.WHAT SUPPORTS ME?

1 THE MAGICIAN

The Magician tells us that Beverly is good at making her own magick. Her personal power and her will keep her healthy. The tools and interests she has also support her health, like the blood-level monitor she uses, and the craftwork she enjoys.

12.WHAT HINDERS MY HEALING?

KING OF SWORDS

Beverly may be over-rationalizing regarding her illnesses and letting that distract her from the healing process or from following her diet and other prescriptions more strictly. She's worrying and thinking about it all too much.

13.WHAT HELPS MY HEALING?

ACE OF COINS

This card points out the healing power of Beverly's many small business interests, like the doll making, story writing, painting and all her other money-making ventures. They keep her interested and feeling alive, which helps the healing process.

14. WHAT DO I NEED TO LET GO?

5 OF COINS (REVERSED)

The 5 of Coins usually reveals a true handicap that must be adapted to because it cannot be overcome. Reversed, this card tells us that some perceived handicap or lack of ability can be overcome, and that Beverly needs to let go of the idea that she has this handicap, or the self-perception that she is handicapped by her illness.

15. WHAT DO I NEED TO HONOUR?

14 TEMPERANCE (REVERSED)

The reversal of the Temperance card can act as an exclamation mark to emphasize the need for balance and moderation. It can also indicate the opposite: a need to recognize the imbalances in your life and the growth and opportunities they bring. It's up to Beverly to meditate on this card and what it means to her.

16. WHAT DO I NEED TO DO TODAY?

KNIGHT OF WANDS

This Knight advises a departure from routine into something completely different. It takes an act of will to move in an unexpected direction.

17. WHAT DO I NEED TO DO TOMORROW?

3 THE EMPRESS (REVERSED)

Beverly needs to take stock of what she has and what she hasn't. There is a problem or lessening in abundance that needs to be addressed. Maybe some resource can no longer be counted on. It may be her own physical energy as she grows older. The Empress is a powerful nurturing card, which gives birth to new projects and ideas. Reversed, she indicates that Beverly is best served by drawing her nurturing energy inward toward herself and this medical situation, rather than expanding outward and putting energy into external pursuits.

chapter six
Freeing the Spirit

Arthur Edward Waite, creator of the popular Rider-Waite deck, considered the divinatory use of the tarot to be a veil that hid the tarot's true meaning and purpose. Through the practices of scrying and meditation, you can move beyond descriptive definitions of the symbols to a more esoteric plane of clarity and understanding. This last chapter includes guides to scrying, meditation and basic tarot altar construction, all designed to develop and nurture your connection to the infinite and the divine. Let's move beyond the physical and mental and venture forth into spiritual life planning.

Scrying

Scrying can be performed with or without asking a specific question, and describes a process whereby you seek new information. It means to see from a distance. There are many ways to scry. You can gaze at water, a crystal, a candle flame, melted wax, a black mirror, clouds, smoke, fire and, of course, tarot cards. It takes hours of silent practice and people often lose patience with it before achieving any result. Like anything else, practice makes perfect; in the case of scrying the practice consists of sitting still in silence in a darkened room. For some, sitting still and remaining silent, without music, light and something visual to entertain them, is simply an impossibility. It can be hard to ratchet down the input to one dimly seen tarot card, crystal, candle flame or even nothing. No wonder scrying is a rare art.

Universal Knowledge

There exists in cultures and traditions worldwide a concept of eternal knowledge, or records of the sum total of human experience, called the Akashic records. There is even a modern, scientific explanation of knowledge stored within the genetic code or cellular memory. Scrying is a method of accessing this universal library of all knowledge past, present and future.

Meditation

The process whereby you reflect on the new information gained from scrying for deeper understanding and clarity of purpose is meditation. Meditation is more popular than scrying and has all sorts of purposes, ranging from simply calming the mind and relaxing the body to understanding one's place in the universe. Use the tarot to unlock the secrets of the universe and find true peace. Meditate on the cards you find peaceful and enjoyable, like the Sun and the 10 of Cups, by thinking of them throughout the day or whenever faced with stress.

Meditation Magick

Without trying to accomplish any specific goal, light a candle and simply stare at a card from your deck. Open yourself to the mystery. It takes time and practice to let go of desire and the intellect and dive inward, deep into the divine well of eternal knowledge. Sometimes meditation reveals deep meanings, stemming back from childhood associations with the symbols, and sometimes we receive information or tasks in regard to our life purpose, the meaning of life or our eternal identity.

Scrying the Tarot

Scrying is an esoteric science. Like any scientific discipline it has rules and principles, although it takes patient practice to truly understand them. There are lots of reasons for scrying the tarot cards. You may want to work with each of the major arcana to study in depth and learn each archetype more fully. You may be working the majors in your life and find you are stuck on one card for a long time.

In your reading and layouts, you may find a card or two that fills you with dread, or that you can't relate to, and you want to find out why. Or you may be working through a particular energy in your life and find a card that models it. Scry that card to better understand the challenges and reality it depicts.

Begin your scrying practice with this guided session that encourages you to access the archetype in your own 'hardwired' cellular pattern.

As you gain practice with scrying, and are able to sit for 20 minutes at a time, you will be able to blank your mind completely and open yourself to the collective subconscious or universal mind without thought or prompting. The idea is to let go of all things physical in order to enter beyond the veil into the subtle and spiritual – as though you are getting out of the car so that you can enter the house.

STONE AGE SCRYING

Before written history, perhaps even before language and oral tradition, when life was a daily struggle for survival, how were things learned? How was knowledge passed on? I submit that people had to be much more aware of themselves and their surroundings than we are today, when danger and threat are so far removed from our daily existence. People scryed the sky with their eyes, the air with their nose and ears; they existed for most of the time in a deeply aware state of consciousness, alert to all and any information. Nowadays we experience information overload and purposely dull our senses of perception. Take this opportunity to reawaken your ancient senses of perception. Listen to the wisdom of your ancestors.

SCRY THE SYMBOLS

A great card to scry for the first time is your birth or year card.

- Your birth card bears a major life lesson or purpose that you will find yourself returning to throughout life. To find your birth card, add together the single digits of your birth date, for example 19th January 1963 (19/1/63) would be 1 + 9 + 1 + 6 + 3 = 20 Judgement. If your total is greater than 22 (The Fool), then add together the digits again to reduce the total. For example, 33 would become 3 + 3 = 6 The Lovers.
- Once you have your card to scry, sit in a silent, darkened room with one candle or a lightbox illuminating the card.
- Breathe deeply, hold, release. Continue to breathe deeply and regularly.
- Focus your eyes on the card.
- Unfocus and let your mind wander.
- Narrow the focus down onto the card again.
- Now relax the eyes and let the eyelids droop.
- Open your third eye (intuition or psychic vision) to the archetype in the card.
- Observe the pictures and patterns that flow into your mind. Either write them down or speak them into a voice recorder or your phone.
- Ask the following questions, allowing several minutes each for the answers to form:

  What do my ancestors say?
  What does the Akashic records say? Why am I here now?
  What do I need to know about this card?
  What do I know about this from before times (search within your soul)?

SCRYING THE CHARIOT REVELATIONS

Just as soon as you think you understand a card fully, you will learn a new meaning for it. See what wisdom you can glean from the Chariot.

While in the Chariot, my feet are not on the ground.
My body is the vehicle given to me by the Goddess. It will take me wherever I desire, on the royal road to happiness or the highway to hell. It is my choice. I steer the Chariot.
Like a car destined for the junkyard, this body is destined for the grave. The body can only go so far in expressing the spirit.
Will bent in the shape of desire has brought me here.
Watch where you direct the Chariot, for it will surely carry you there.

Meditation

Now that you have scryed deeper understanding with your tarot, you can integrate this new knowledge into your everyday life through meditation. Scrying is difficult because you have to let go of everything external, even the subtle mind, and journey deeper to the cellular, unconscious level. Meditation should be easy, pleasant, relaxing and serene. Actively engage the mind in meditation while keeping it open to communication from the higher self at the subconscious level.

FOUR-PHASE GUIDED MEDITATION

Use this meditation to understand how the truth and energy of a card acts in your life, using the same card that you used for the scrying exercise. Take your time at each of the four stations. Allow yourself to visualize the scenes completely. Meditate on the details supplied by your mind's eye as well as the details on the card. Sit comfortably in a quiet calm place, free from distractions. You might want to play some tonal music or something beautiful that helps you relax. Place your tarot card where you can see it easily without holding it. Keep gazing at it throughout the meditation.

- Journey to the East to watch the sun rise. See the flowers open, feel the light breeze dance on your skin. You meet a being of Air. This being shows you how to see this card in your life. Accept a gift from the East.

- Journey to the South at high noon. See the dry sand dunes and feel the heat. You meet a being of Fire. This being shows you how this card transforms your life. Accept a gift from the South.

- Journey to the West and watch the sun set. See the river flowing and feel all else grow still. You meet a being of Water. This being shows you the natural flow of this card in your life. Accept a gift from the West.

- Journey to the North at midnight. See the dark shadows and feel the piercing cold. You meet a being of Earth. This being shows you the stillness and gravity of this card in your life. Accept a gift from the North.

- Return to the here and now. Gather up your lessons and gifts. Thank the beings you met along the journey.

- Write down your realizations.

QUEEN OF SWORDS REALIZATIONS

When you feel scared or panicked by events, when you're in a bad mood or just feel overwhelmed by negative thoughts, consciously verbalize these thoughts in terms of a tarot archetype.

I am the Queen of Swords when...
I stand up to the woman who is making
me redundant and am escorted from the
building because of it.
I drastically reduce my expenses so that
I can pursue my dreams instead of
running after another 'job'.
I speak my truth even though you may not
like it.
I do the dirty, nasty, difficult, tedious jobs
that no one else will.
I resign myself to the fact that I will
always be alone.
I spray poison on my weeds instead of
pulling them.
I cut ties to people and past events that
are not good for me.

MODERN MEDITATION

I grew up with an idea of meditation as something old bearded men did high up in the Himalayas. To find out the meaning of life, people like me would have to climb the mountains and receive some unintelligible message that we would then spend the rest of our lives puzzling over, but never understanding. I have since come to realize that a hot bathtub is much more conducive to meditation than a cold mountaintop. It's whatever works for you: the calmest time of day or night, a pleasant grove in the woods, or a bench in the garden. You may also want to use music that engages your mind just enough to let the meditative part of it wander unhindered.

Deity Decks

Most decks have religious or divine symbolism such as the archangels in the Rider-Waite deck, the Buddha in the Zerner-Farber deck, the lilies in the Master deck and the lotus flower in the Goddess Tarot deck. There are many religion- or spirituality-based decks available in both the 78-card format and non-standard formats. Thus, wonderfully, there are many pictures or icons of deities to work with.

PRAYER AND WORSHIP

Using the card as a picture, you can frame it or keep it loose and make it the centrepiece of an altar where you offer incense every day. Using a picture helps keep your sense of sight involved in the spiritual act of prayer and worship. Focusing on a tarot card also keeps your mind fully engaged because of all the meanings and mindfulness you have attached to the particular card, whether it is a picture of a particular deity or symbolizes an ideal that you hold dear.

The ancient Vedic philosophy of achintya-beda-abeda tattva nullifies the argument that worshipping demi-gods and goddesses and nature spirits is idolatry. God is unlimited and unlimitedly merciful. He has infinite energies and is present everywhere. He is simultaneously at one with and different from His energies. Therefore, offering incense daily to a picture of Juno for a harmonious wedding is no different from worshipping God in church. Note that this is a simple example to illustrate a complex theological position that is otherwise beyond the scope of this tarot book.

TAROT WORSHIP

It's important to stress that by working with a picture of Odin or a Koala or Athena, you are not therefore stating that this is the one true god. Setting up an altar with one of these cards shows honour and respect, as well as a desire for that energy or ideal or archetype. If God is everywhere, He is also in this tarot card and so it deserves worship. Building a tarot altar and offering respect to your chosen deity creates sacred space in your home and in your life. It raises your consciousness, making your life more holy and spiritual.

Altar Construction

Create an altar to your deity by adding a card or cards to your existing sacred space, or construct a special altar from scratch as the spirit moves you. There are several types of altar that you can create in your home. Choose the one that best suits you.

BASIC

The Basic altar is used for simplicity, if there are space considerations, if you are allergic to incense, or have any other reason not to want an elaborate altar.

- Find a small space with some surface at table height that you can make sacred and use for no other purpose.
- Lay down a nice cloth on your surface to help define your sacred altar and give it boundaries.
- Place your deity picture where you can see it clearly and it won't get knocked over.
- Put a plastic flower, a gemstone or some other permanent gift in front of the picture.
- Set aside a few moments to 'talk' to your deity every day.

ELABORATE

An elaborate altar will be filled with items that are meaningful to you and that honour your deity.

- Set aside a portion of a room as sacred. Choose a surface with enough room for all your items, plus a 'working' space.
- Place a card of your deity where you can see it. You may want to add a large framed picture of your deity in addition to the card or cards.
- Some good general additions to your altar are a fire-safe incense burner, such as a bowl of sand or gravel, or an incense holder with a tile or metal plate beneath it for Air; a fire-safe candle holder for Fire; a glass or bowl of water (change it daily) for Water; a dish of earth or salt for Earth; a living plant or fresh cut flowers for Spirit.
- You may want to add other items that strengthen the spiritual connection you feel with your deity, such as a stone or feather you found on a special day, the colours or decorations of holy days, gifts your deity has sent to you, gifts you like to give to your deity, etc.

PURPOSIVE

This tarot altar is especially meant to attract love into your life, using the Master Tarot's pictures of Jesus' life and teachings (see opposite).

- Set aside a sacred space.
- Lay out the cards you want to work with. If possible, prop them up where you can see them all easily. If you choose to work with many cards, write down their purpose and your reasoning so you can keep them fresh in your mind day after day.
- Place items related to your purpose, such as red and white hearts, roses, 'Love is . . .' statements, things that make you feel loved and loving.
- Light a red candle daily for Love, or a green or pink candle to symbolize the heart chakra, and place it in front of the cards.
- Offer respect and praise. 'Talk' to your higher power. Affirm your desire and purpose – for the greatest good of all and for your own greatest good.
- Ask for the miracle.
- Gaze at the cards and listen with your heart. Amen.

SACRED CIRCLE OF PROTECTION

Perform the following exercise daily or weekly:

- Light incense and candle. Sprinkle some water and salt. Offer fresh flowers or some small gift or token like chocolate or coins.
- Offer praise and devotion. State affirmations.
- Listen within your heart for an answer or instruction.
- Thank your deity and release the circle (see page 15).

DEITY CARDS FROM THE MASTER TAROT

34 Knock: opens the door and starts the prayer process

36 Prayer: energizes and defines the altar space as a prayer medium

I The Son of Man: a picture of Jesus

27 Total Faith: an expression of trust and praise

X The Miracle: opens the possibility

XIV Love one another: the miracle desired; love

Absoluter Glaube
Total Faith

GODDESS DECKS

Goddess decks come with a description of the energies and 'purposes' of the Goddesses, like Lucina for renewal, Mawu for power, Kuan Yin for self-sacrifice, and Laxmi for prosperity. The cards of the deck you choose to work with will have special meaning for you whether it be the energies of Norse mythology, the Native Americans, Australian Dreamtime or Celtic wisdom.

Index